WINNING THE INVISIBLE WAR

MICHAEL YOUSSEF

HARVEST HOUSE PUBLISHERS
EUGENE, OREGON

Unless otherwise indicated, Scripture verses are taken from the Holy Bible, New International Version®, NIV®. Copyright © 1973, 1978, 1984, 2011 by Biblica, Inc.® Used with permission of Zondervan. All rights reserved worldwide. www.zondervan.com. The "NIV" and "New International Version" are trademarks registered in the United States Patent and Trademark Office by Biblica, Inc.®

Verses marked NKJV or attributed to the New King James Version are taken from the New King James Version®. Copyright © 1982 by Thomas Nelson. Used with permission. All rights reserved.

Verses attributed to the New American Standard Bible are taken from the (NASB®) New American Standard Bible®, Copyright © 1960, 1971, 1977, 1995, 2020 by The Lockman Foundation. Used by permission. All rights reserved. lockman.org.

Verses marked KJV or attributed to the King James Version and verses attributed to the American Standard Version are in the public domain.

Published in association with Don Gates of the literary agency,
The Gates Group, www.the-gates-group.com

Cover design by Kyler Dougherty

Cover images © kyoshino, studiocasper / Getty Images

Interior design by KUHN Design Group

For bulk, special sales, or ministry purchases, please call 1-800-547-8979.
Email: CustomerService@hhpbooks.com

This logo is a federally registered trademark of the Hawkins Children's LLC. Harvest House Publishers, Inc., is the exclusive licensee of this trademark.

Winning the Invisible War
Copyright © 2025 by Michael Youssef
Published by Harvest House Publishers
Eugene, Oregon 97408
www.harvesthousepublishers.com

ISBN 978-0-7369-9266-4 (pbk)
ISBN 978-0-7369-9267-1 (eBook)

Library of Congress Control Number: 2025930240

No part of this book may be used or reproduced in any manner for the purpose of training artificial intelligence technologies or systems.

All rights reserved. No part of this publication may be reproduced, stored in a retrieval system, or transmitted in any form or by any means—electronic, mechanical, digital, photocopy, recording, or any other—except for brief quotations in printed reviews, without the prior permission of the publisher.

Printed in the United States of America

25 26 27 28 29 30 31 32 33 / BP / 10 9 8 7 6 5 4 3 2 1

CONTENTS

Introduction: The Struggle We Face 5

1. Assault from the Outside 11

2. The Battle Within 35

3. Angels and Demons 53

4. Armored for Battle 71

5. Vigilance in Wartime 95

6. The Blessings of Surrender 113

7. Know Your Enemy 133

8. Wielding Your Sword 151

9. Recovery from Failure 173

10. Don't Forget to Breathe....................... 193

    Conclusion: Stand Firm to the End 211

    Notes 217

Whenever we see God at work, there will be opposition and warfare. There will be peril and risk. But it's an exciting way to live—and there are unimaginable rewards for all who fight in the army of the Lord.

INTRODUCTION

THE STRUGGLE WE FACE

On February 24, 2022, Russian dictator Vladimir Putin sent thousands of troops into neighboring Ukraine—a massive escalation of the Russian-Ukrainian War. But long before that military invasion, Russia had been waging an *invisible* war against Ukraine and Western nations.

Tech journalist Andy Greenberg reports that Russia has engaged in cyberwarfare against the West since 2015. Russian hackers have crippled hospitals and power grids, shut corporate operations, and spread panic in government institutions—not only in Ukraine but around the world, including the United States.

These attacks should have triggered an international response. Instead, Greenberg said, all the governments around the world—except Ukraine—pretended nothing happened. Russia got away with its crimes because the war it waged was *invisible*. This lack of consequences, Greenberg said, "invited Russia to just keep going."[1]

In much the same way, Satan and his demonic agents are now waging an invisible war against the forces of God and the entire human race. Many people—including many Christians—pretend that there is no war. They even deny that Satan exists because they can't detect his presence with their physical senses.

But the invisible war is real. It's raging every day all around us and within us. This war destroys many lives, day after day—yet we cannot see the enemy with our own eyes. This war brings disorder and division to our society—yet few people know where our invisible enemy lurks. The prophets and apostles and Jesus himself explained to us the strategies and tactics of our invisible foe—yet we continually find ourselves vulnerable to the enemy's plans and schemes.

That is why I have written *Winning the Invisible War*. I want you to see with the eyes of your soul and spirit what your physical eyes cannot see. I want you to understand the nature of the battle we face and the plans of our enemy. I want you to be a victor, not a victim, of our invisible struggle against Satan and his demonic agents in the world.

SATAN IS REAL

The more you want to be effective for the Lord, the more Satan will intensify his assault. Satan always revs up his attack machine against those who want to grow deeper in the faith.

You might think, "Well, I'll just drift along in my Christian life. I don't want any conflict with Satan. I'll be a complacent, third-rate Christian—and that way Satan will leave me alone." But do you really prefer mediocrity and defeat over the adventure of knowing and serving Jesus?

It's true that Christians can and do play at being Christians. Churches can play at being God's church. It's easy to be a pretend Christian, a pretend church. And if you choose to be a pretend Christian, Satan may well leave you alone.

A Christian can go to church and talk the talk and sing the songs—and never be truly serious about a genuine relationship with Jesus. A church can have a popular preacher, lots of activities and programs, the best worship music—and never be serious about God's kingdom.

A church or a Christian who just pretends is a spiritually dead corpse. Satan won't bother a corpse. But why would you want to be a corpse?

Whenever we see God at work, there will be opposition and warfare. There will be peril and risk. But it's an exciting way to live—and there are unimaginable rewards for all who fight in the army of the Lord.

Satan is crafty and deceptive. One of his most successful deceptions is the widespread claim that he doesn't exist at all, that belief in a literal devil is mere superstition.

According to a nationwide survey of adults who call themselves Christians, 59 percent said they somewhat or strongly agree that Satan "is not a living being but is a symbol of evil." Only a minority of Christians—35 percent—said they somewhat or strongly believe that Satan is real. The remaining participants couldn't say what they believe.[2]

THE IDENTITY OF SATAN

To believe that Satan doesn't exist, you must deny many key passages of Scripture. Jesus said he saw Satan fall from heaven (see Luke 10:18). He spoke directly to Satan when he was tempted in the wilderness (see Matthew 4; Mark 1; and Luke 4).

Satan is depicted in Scripture from Genesis to Revelation. Disguised as a serpent, Satan deceived Adam and Eve. He was the source of Job's torments. He was the accuser of the nation of Judah and its high priest (see Zechariah 3). God, speaking through Ezekiel, said to Satan:

> You were anointed as a guardian cherub,
>   for so I ordained you.
> You were on the holy mount of God;
>   you walked among the fiery stones.
> You were blameless in your ways
>   from the day you were created
>   till wickedness was found in you (Ezekiel 28:14-15).

The book of Hebrews tells us that, on the cross, Jesus shattered "the power of him who holds the power of death—that is, the devil" (Hebrews 2:14). Paul tells us that Satan hinders God's servants (1 Thessalonians 2:18), hinders the gospel (2 Corinthians 4:4), sets traps for believers (1 Timothy 3:7), and disguises himself as an angel of light (2 Corinthians 11:14). Paul calls Satan "the god of this age" (2 Corinthians 4:4) and "the ruler of the kingdom of the air" (Ephesians 2:2)—which means that Satan controls the systems of this world, such as the United Nations and the World Economic Forum, which may one day be Satan's tools for imposing a one-world government on all nations—a government ruled by the Antichrist.

In Jude 1:9, Satan contends with the archangel Michael. And John tells us that the whole world is under Satan's control (1 John 5:19).

Jesus depicts Satan in several parables, including the parable of the sower, the parable of the weeds (or tares), and the parable of the strong man. Jesus tells us that Satan "was a murderer from the beginning, not holding to the truth, for there is no truth in him. When he lies, he speaks his native language, for he is a liar and the father of lies" (John 8:44). Jesus also called Satan "the prince of this world" (John 12:31; 16:11). The Gospel of John reveals that Satan personally inspired Judas to betray Jesus (John 13:2).

The Bible is emphatically clear: Satan is not a metaphor. He's *real*. Jesus has confronted him face-to-face. Satan and his agents are invisibly present and active in the world around us. We need to understand who Satan is, how he behaves, and what his strategies are.

OUR INVISIBLE STRUGGLE

Paul's warning is timely—and timeless: "Our struggle is not against flesh and blood, but against the rulers, against the authorities, against the powers of this dark world and against the spiritual forces of evil in the heavenly realms" (Ephesians 6:12). When Paul speaks of "our struggle," he uses a Greek word that suggests a wrestling match, a battle at close quarters.

Our enemy is a deceiver who doesn't fight fairly. He and his subordinate demons—"the spiritual forces of evil in the heavenly realms"—routinely lie and break every rule. Paul wants us to understand that Satan's goal is to destroy the church of Jesus Christ.

Never forget that while we Christians squabble among ourselves over doctrinal disputes or the color of the carpet in the church sanctuary, Satan's army is highly disciplined, highly motivated, and well organized. The rulers, authorities, and powers of this dark world are obedient to the chain of command.

Satan's forces are intensely interested in human affairs, and they have infiltrated the political systems of Earth. You might think that Satan and his agents have only taken control of oppressive authoritarian regimes like those of Russia, Iran, Cuba, North Korea, and Communist China. But no, the army of Satan has countless agents in our so-called "Western democracies," manipulating our leaders, spreading lies, and infecting all levels of government with satanic ideologies.

We dare not ignore the threat we face. Instead, let's look to our Commander, the Lord Jesus, who alone is powerful enough to defeat Satan.

DON'T BE A DRAFT DODGER!

The Vietnam War caused deep divisions in American society in the 1960s and 1970s. The war was so controversial that vast numbers of young American men resisted the draft. Many fled to Canada rather than be sent to Vietnam. Official records show that the government classified about 570,000 American men as draft offenders.[3]

One of the leading figures of the anti-draft movement was folk singer Phil Ochs, who performed a satirical tune called "Draft Dodger Rag." In the song, a young man reports to the draft board and lists all the reasons he can't go to Vietnam, including a ruptured spleen, bad eyes, flat feet, and an addiction to drugs.[4] Many Christians are like the draft dodger in that song. They have a hundred excuses for not serving in God's army. They are Christian draft dodgers, refusing to report for duty in the invisible war.

Christian draft dodgers aren't interested in putting on the full armor of God. After all, why would anyone need to wear armor if he's fled the battlefield? But the true soldier in Christ's army knows the joy that comes from putting on the full armor of God. All we have to do is suit up and then let our Commander fight for us.

Unimaginable rewards await us at the end of our adventure. The greatest joy belongs to those who have fought the invisible war to its inevitable conclusion. If you go into battle wearing the armor of God, in the strength and might of your Commander, you can't lose. Victory is assured. And the greater the victory, the greater your eternal joy will be.

So get set for adventure and turn the page. With eyes of faith, guided by God's Word, let's report for duty and claim the victory in the invisible war.

1

ASSAULT FROM THE OUTSIDE

Please don't let Satan frighten you. In fact, the central theme of this book is that we should be bold and courageous as we fight our spiritual battles. In the coming chapters, I'll give you the tools to be victorious in our war against Satan. I will show you again and again that the Lord who is in us, the Lord who leads us, is greater than Satan. Victory is a matter of knowing how to lay hold of God's power for the battles of this life.

ASSAULT FROM THE OUTSIDE

In 2023, students at the B.M. Williams Primary School, an elementary school in Chesapeake, Virginia, got to attend their first After-School Satan Club, sponsored by the local Satanic Temple. The American Civil Liberties Union praised the first meeting as "a victory for free speech and religious liberty."

Members of the Satanic Temple organized the After-School Satan Club in response to Good News Clubs, sponsored by Child Evangelism Fellowship. According to *The Washington Post*, the Satan Club organizers "point out that Christian evangelical groups already have infiltrated the lives of America's children through after-school religious programming in public schools, and they appear determined to give young students a choice: Jesus or Satan."

The *Post* quotes Satanic Temple cofounder Doug Mesner as saying, "It's critical that children understand that there are multiple perspectives on all issues, and that they have a choice in how they think." The Satanic Temple claims not to believe in the existence of Satan or any other supernatural being. Mesner asserts that Satan is merely a "metaphorical construct."[1]

Mesner and his fellow "rational" Satanists are the fulfillment of C.S. Lewis's prophetic words in *The Screwtape Letters*, in which the demon Screwtape says, "When the humans disbelieve in our existence we lose all the pleasing results of direct terrorism and we make no magicians. On the other hand, when they believe in us we cannot make them materialists and skeptics—at least not yet...If once we can produce our perfect work—the Materialist Magician, the man, not using, but veritably worshipping what he vaguely calls 'Forces' while denying the existence of 'spirits'—then the end of the war will be in sight."[2]

Screwtape has achieved his goal. The members of the Satanic Temple perfectly fit Lewis's definition of a "Materialist Magician." They invoke the name of Satan while denying his existence. They claim to help children think rationally while labeling these clubs with the emblem of Satan. Such a masterpiece of deception and delusion could only be hatched by a demonic mind.

We are at war. This is an *invisible* war, a *spiritual* war. And the followers of Satan—even if they don't believe in his existence—are doing his bidding and carrying out his commands. They are targeting your children and grandchildren for destruction.

A CULT HAS CAPTURED OUR CULTURE

During fiscal year 2021–2022, the Massachusetts Department of Children and Families reported that more than 9,700 children were placed in its custody.[3] Many of these children are languishing in state custody because there are not enough foster homes to go around. As one social worker told Boston's Channel 5, "The kids, they have no place to go. They're walking around with garbage bags filled with their clothes, wondering where they're going to go night to night."[4]

You would think that nothing would be more important than finding foster homes for children who have suffered from abuse or neglect or loss. Yet there is one thing that the Massachusetts foster care bureaucracy prizes even more than the welfare of children: ideological purity.

You are undoubtedly aware of the secular-left cult of gender ideology. And yes, I chose the word "cult" with care. Dr. Az Hakeem of Great Britain, a Fellow of the Royal College of Psychiatrists and the author of *Trans: Exploring Gender Identity and Gender Dysphoria*, has said, "Gender ideology is made up. It's a social construct. It's a cult belief…The worst thing we can do is presume it's a medical condition…It's not."[5]

And Kathleen Hayes, who survived more than two decades in a mind-controlling cult, also calls radical gender ideology a cult in which young people are "transformed seemingly overnight into mouthpieces of incomprehensible jargon and vitriol…I use the word 'cult' not as an insult, but because it fits."[6]

The gender ideology cult has had a destructive impact on the policies and practices of the Massachusetts Department of Children and Families. When a Catholic couple, Michael and Catherine "Kitty" Burke, applied to become foster parents, the department sent a social worker to interview them. The social worker asked how the Burkes felt about fostering children who identified as lesbian, gay, bisexual, trans, or queer.

The Burkes said they would love any child unconditionally, but the child would "need to live a chaste life," and they didn't approve of medically altering a child who identified as "transgender." They also expressed hesitation about using so-called "preferred pronouns." Because of those answers, the Burkes' application was denied by the Department of Children and Families. The Burkes have filed a lawsuit, charging the department with violating their First Amendment rights.[7]

An overwhelming majority of Americans oppose radical gender identity ideology.[8] Yet the Massachusetts Department of Children and Families will only accept foster parents who submit to the cult view of gender. Like so many segments of our society, this arm of the government is determined to impose cultlike standards on children and parents.

The cult of radical gender ideology has overwhelmed our schools (from kindergarten through university levels), the teachers' unions, collegiate sports, our news media, Hollywood, and much of our political establishment. President Biden, on his first day in office, signed Executive Order 13988, forcing schools to give men who call themselves "women" access to women's sports teams, bathrooms, and locker rooms.[9] Because of the radical gender cult, no woman or girl in America could feel safe in these women's spaces.

Even though President Biden's successor, President Trump, has reversed Executive Order 13988 and many other policies of the radical gender cult, the satanic forces that lobbied for these policies still wield power and influence in our society. They are still targeting your children and grandchildren for spiritual destruction, and they will not accept defeat. They will not go away quietly.

DON'T BE DECEIVED

The radical gender cult has even infiltrated the practice of medicine. When you sign in at your doctor's office, hospital, or medical lab, you will be asked your "gender identity" and you'll be offered such options as "Agender," "Transgender," "Genderqueer," and "Nonbinary." The American Medical Association, the Children's Hospital Association, and the American Academy of Pediatrics have been fully persuaded by the radical gender cult, and now endorse the sexual mutilation of minor children with puberty blockers, hormones, and experimental gender surgeries, including surgically removing girls' breasts and boys' genitals.[10]

The gender theorists tell us that biological sex is irrelevant to our identity. They claim that our sexuality is a blank slate upon which we can write any identity we choose. They "gaslight" us and tell us that our sex is "assigned at birth" by the doctors who delivered us, when it is obvious to any rational person that one's anatomical sex is *observed* by the doctor, not "assigned." I am convinced that this cult ideology is all part of a satanic strategy to shatter families and destroy young souls.

Genesis 1:27 tells us that God made us, both male and female, in his image. And 1 Corinthians 6:19 tells us that our bodies are temples of the Holy Spirit. Our manhood or womanhood is a gift from God. Our masculinity or femininity is *not* something we should disregard or disfigure or try to rewrite.

Since the beginning of time, Satan has tried to upend and usurp God's creation, including the human beings God created. Satan continually tempts us to reject God's design for our lives. God creates; Satan destroys. God gives life; Satan inflicts death. God blesses; Satan curses.

When Adam fell, the human race and all of creation came under a curse. One aspect of that curse, I believe, is that it caused many people to experience confusion and distortion in their identity and sexuality. Today, evil people, led by Satan, are working overtime to normalize these corrupted sexual identities—and seduce more and more confused people into their cult.

If you look all around our culture, it becomes obvious that evil forces that used to lurk in the shadows are now out in the open. Their satanic goals and power are on full display. These forces of evil are the foot soldiers of the Father of Lies, and that is why they spread an ideology of lies. They lie just as Satan lies. They want to deceive well-meaning but undiscerning people. That is their goal.

I don't want you to be deceived. That's why I am giving you examples and naming names. I want you to be aware of the invisible enemy that has targeted you and your family. I want you to be aware of the invisible war that is being fought all around you—from outside you and from within you. I want you to be well defended against the powerful satanic deception that pervades and rules this world.

Let me give you a few examples of how Satan is assaulting us all from the outside.

SATANIC ATTACKS ON OUR CHILDREN

First, *the child indoctrination movement* is a demonic stronghold. This movement can be found in both the public schools and in the entertainment industry. I could offer hundreds of examples, but let's just look at two.

Public school teachers and librarians are working hand-in-hand with cross-dressing entertainers—so-called "drag queens"—to indoctrinate our children into accepting sexual perversion. Events called "Drag Queen Story Hour" first began in San Francisco in 2015. At these events, a man dressed in a wig, garish makeup, fake body contours, and a colorful gown reads books to young children in a womanish voice. The books have titles like *Bye, Bye Binary*, *The Gender Wheel*, and *They, She, He, Easy as ABC*.

Years ago, when I first heard about a "Drag Queen Story Hour" in San Francisco, I thought, *Well, that's San Francisco for you!* But I underestimated the evil forces behind that first event. Since then, "Drag Queen Story Hour" has spread across America, and thousands of children from preschool age on up are being brainwashed into denying and defiling their God-given sexuality.[11] Drag Story Hour is now a national organization. Its website proudly proclaims:

What Is Drag Story Hour?

It's just what it sounds like! Storytellers using the art of drag to read books to kids in libraries, schools, and bookstores.

> DSH captures the imagination and play of the gender fluidity of childhood and gives kids glamorous, positive, and unabashedly queer role models.
>
> In spaces like this, kids are able to see people who defy rigid gender restrictions and imagine a world where everyone can be their authentic selves![12]

How pervasive is the influence of this organization? At the bottom of its website, Drag Story Hour lists "some organizations we've worked with," including Disney, PBS, HBO, Facebook, Google, Hulu, Microsoft, Spotify, and Home Chef.[13] Why do you think these organizations, along with countless schools and public libraries, want to recruit little children into an "unabashedly queer" lifestyle? What kind of mind is ultimately behind this assault on the innocence of our children?

The second example of the child indoctrination movement (and it pains me to say this) is the Walt Disney Company. The founder of the company, Walt Disney, was a flawed man in many ways, but he professed a strong faith in God and a strong desire to produce wholesome entertainment for the entire family.[14] I'm sure he would be appalled to see the morally toxic fare his company spews out today.

The Disney Company has made no secret of the LGBTQ+ agenda in many of its products aimed at children. Some recent examples:

- *Star Wars Resistance*, an animated series that aired from 2018 to 2020 on the Disney Channel, featuring LGBTQ characters

- A short Pixar animated film titled *Out* on Disney+ in 2020, about a boy who hides his gay identity from his parents

- The animated series *The Owl House*, which ran on The Disney Channel from 2020 through 2023, featuring several LGBTQ characters

- *The Proud Family: Louder and Prouder*, which premiered on Disney+ in 2022, featuring assorted LGBTQ themes and characters

- *Strange World*, a 2022 animated film featuring Disney's first gay lead character

- *Lightyear*, a 2022 animated theatrical release from Pixar and Walt Disney Pictures, which features the studio's first on-screen same-sex kiss

- *Elemental*, a 2023 Pixar-Disney movie with a "nonbinary" character who uses "they/them pronouns"[15]

In 2022, video from an online Disney "employee diversity and inclusion meeting" was leaked to the media. In the video, Disney television animation executive producer Latoya Raveneau (*The Proud Family: Louder and Prouder*) said, "In my little pocket of Proud Family Disney TVA, the showrunners were super welcoming…to my not-at-all-secret gay agenda…[I felt a] sense of 'I don't have to be afraid to have these two characters kiss in the background.' I was just, wherever I could, adding queerness…No one would stop me, and no one was trying to stop me."[16]

Please understand, God loves LGBTQ people and so do I. The concern I am raising here comes not out of hatred or so-called "homophobia," but from my conviction that no one should ever try to sexualize children or rob them of their innocence. Jesus himself warns of God's dire judgment against anyone who "causes one of these little ones… to stumble." So I pray for revival and repentance to take hold of the

Walt Disney Company. I pray that God would raise up believers who would steer the company toward using its power and influence to enrich the lives of children instead of indoctrinating them.

These are just two examples of how Satan has targeted our children for moral and spiritual destruction.

"WHEN WOKEISM REPLACES COMMON SENSE"

Second, *the public education system* is rapidly being infiltrated and even conquered by satanic ideologies. This should chill the marrow of every citizen, especially parents and grandparents. Former federal prosecutor Andrew C. McCarthy warns against "the conversion of the nation's public schools into ideological-indoctrination factories that peddle woke, race-obsessed anti-Americanism" and he urges parents to "hold school boards accountable in local elections."[17]

Kaylee McGhee White of the *Washington Examiner* observes, "Bureaucrats and union lobbyists running the public education system aren't actually interested in educating or caring for students… [Woke instructional materials have] taken over public schools' curricula. From the ahistorical *1619 Project* to the *Gender Unicorn*, leftist ideology is running amok in our public classrooms, and students are suffering as a result."[18]

White observes that reading and mathematics proficiency scores are plummeting, and American students are lagging behind students in other countries. "In California," she writes, "the average eighth grader has the mathematical proficiency of a fifth grader. One would think this lapse in achievement would send off alarm bells in the minds of education leaders. And yet the state's response has been to lower the testing standards for the sake of diversity, equity, and inclusion. This is what happens when wokeism replaces common sense."[19]

Kali Fontanilla was a public school teacher in California who left her job when, she said, "it became clear to me that school officials were obsessed with left-wing indoctrination, and that dissenting voices—like my own—were not welcome." She says that public school officials are single-mindedly imposing on students the notion that (in her words) "America was founded on systemic racism and that our institutions still discriminate against black Americans like me."

She reports that students memorize the "four I's of oppression (institutional, internalized, ideological, and interpersonal)," that students are taught to rank their identities into "intersectional rainbows," and that they are given a "privilege quiz" in which students grade how much they are "marginalized" or "privileged." Because she can no longer do her job in California, Fontanilla and her husband moved to Florida and opened an online K-12 school called Exodus Institute.[20]

You might think, "Well, that's California for you—a neon-blue progressive state. I live in a red state, and I'm sure my kids are being educated, not indoctrinated." Don't be too sure about that. Even public schools in conservative regions have been infiltrated by teachers who are products of the university indoctrination industry. Like our universities, many formerly excellent public schools have been turned into indoctrination factories.

I urge you, if at all possible, to get your children or grandchildren out of the clutches of government-run schools. If you can afford an excellent Christian private school, or if you can homeschool your children or get them into a homeschool co-op, I urge you to do so. I know that privately educating children is a sacrifice of time and money—but the government school alternative requires you to *sacrifice your children* on the altar of satanic ideologies.

If you absolutely have no choice but to keep your children in the public school system, then make sure you are involved. Talk to your children about what they are learning. Volunteer to help in the classroom. Know what books are available in the school library. Attend school board meetings. Defend your children from the cult ideologies that are all around us.

Don't let your children be casualties of the invisible war in our society.

SATAN GOES TO COLLEGE

Third, *the university system* is a stronghold of Satan. The concept of higher learning was invented by Christians in the Middle Ages. The world's first university was founded as a Christian cathedral school at Bologna, Italy, in about 1088. The medieval church soon founded more universities in Oxford, Cambridge, and Paris. Christian scholars taught students how to reason and how to explore the orderly world God had made.

Most of the leading universities in America were founded by Christians. Harvard University was founded by Puritans in 1636 and named for the Puritan clergyman John Harvard. Yale University and Dartmouth were also founded by Puritans. The University of Chicago was founded by Baptists. Brown University, Columbia University, and the College of William and Mary were founded by Anglicans. Princeton was founded by Presbyterians. Duke University was founded by Methodists.

Today, all of these institutions have been largely captured by godless ideologies. Christians founded them, and Satan hijacked them. Satan doesn't have a creative mind, and he can't create a university. He has to infiltrate and take over what God's people have created. So, instead of learning how to reason, today's university students are indoctrinated by tenured radicals into anti-Christian, neo-Marxist ideologies such as "postcolonial theory," "queer theory," and "fat studies."

The mind-virus of "woke" grievance studies has infected every department, including the so-called "hard sciences" of mathematics, physics, and astronomy. An American Mathematical Society blog post asserts that math must be taught as an "intersectional, anti-racist, and class-consciously feminist enterprise" which rejects the "whiteness" of traditional mathematics.[21] Marxist university professors fill young skulls full of mush with the idea that "diversity" means conformity to a cult ideology, that "inclusivity" means intolerance of differing opinions, and that the traditional family equals "patriarchal oppression."

Don't buy into the lie that you or your children *must* go to college to succeed in life. The list of successful people who never earned a college degree includes media figures Mark Burnett and Rush Limbaugh; tech entrepreneurs Bill Gates, Michael Dell, and Larry Ellison; and retail entrepreneurs John Mackey and David Green. If you or your children need a college education to enter a field such as law or medicine, then I urge you to consider an excellent Christian college or university to lay a solid learning foundation *without* godless indoctrination.

WHEN GOOD IS EVIL AND EVIL IS GOOD

Fourth, *the criminal justice system* has been infected by satanic ideologies. The Bible tells us, "The one in authority is God's servant for your good. But if you do wrong, be afraid, for rulers do not bear the sword for no reason. They are God's servants, agents of wrath to bring punishment on the wrongdoer" (Romans 13:4). Today, prosecutors in many leftist cities have turned God's plan for good government on its head.

A prime example is New York City, where District Attorney Alvin Bragg, Jr., lets the "wrongdoers" go free while he prosecutes innocent citizens. I'm reminded of the warning of the prophet Isaiah: "Woe to those who call evil good and good evil, who put darkness for light and light for darkness" (Isaiah 5:20).

Bragg is a pioneering leader of the "progressive prosecution movement," which is rooted in critical race theory.[22] In 2021, Bragg said, "I will not prosecute most petty offenses...I will either dismiss these charges outright or offer the accused person the opportunity to complete a program without ever setting foot in a courtroom." The result, according to the police department data, was that New York City has been overrun by a small number of criminals who are arrested and released hundreds of times without any consequences.[23]

In 2022, Bragg hired Meg Reiss as his chief prosecutor. Her focus was to implement "racial equity reforms" explicitly rooted in critical race theory. She said she would stop treating criminals as "bad dudes"—and she would no longer give "the benefit of the doubt to law enforcement" when police used force against suspects.[24] Meg Reiss wants criminals on the streets, not in prison, saying, "We know incarceration doesn't really solve any problems."[25]

While showing leniency to the vilest criminals, Alvin Bragg and his office prosecuted the innocent. One of the most outrageous cases was Bragg's prosecution of Jose Alba, a bodega clerk in his sixties.

On July 7, 2022, a young man came behind Alba's counter, shouting threats. In the struggle, Alba grabbed a knife and stabbed the assailant, who died of his wounds. Though the police said Alba had acted in self-defense, Bragg wanted to punish Alba for defending himself. He charged Alba with murder, requested bail of $500,000, and had Alba confined to New York's notorious Rikers Island prison. Bragg only dropped the charges after protests from the public and civic leaders.[26]

Bragg's office also prosecuted a Marine veteran named Daniel Penny, who tackled a crazed man who threatened subway riders, screaming "I'm ready to die!" After the struggle, Penny got the man in a chokehold, during which the man died. It turned out that the crazed man had a record of 42 arrests, including four for assault. Penny's fellow subway passengers hailed him as a hero—but Alvin Bragg tried to send him to prison for up to 15 years.

Though the jury acquitted Penny on December 9, 2024, Bragg's prosecution of Penny effectively made New York City subways more dangerous. Less than two weeks after the acquittal, an illegal immigrant set fire to a woman sleeping on a subway car. As she burned to death, witnesses stood by and recorded the horror with their phones, but no one moved to help her or catch the murderer. This response was later called "the Daniel Penny effect," because people feared being prosecuted.[27]

Alvin Bragg is just one of many soft-on-crime prosecutors who are supported by organizations funded by radical-left billionaire George Soros. Others include George Gascón in Los Angeles (who was removed by voters in 2024 because of surging crime rates), Kim Foxx in Chicago, and Larry Krasner in Philadelphia. Reporters Cully Stimson and Zack Smith call this phenomenon "the rogue prosecutor movement" and say it's "an outgrowth of the same radicals that created the Black Lives Matter movement."[28]

A DESTROY-THE-FAMILY AGENDA

Fifth, *radical activism* has all the traits of a satanic strategy. We have seen the rise of radical activist movements that are bent on tearing down our civilization. Examples include: Antifa, which uses fascist violence to advance a supposedly "anti-fascist" cause; Black Lives Matter (BLM), the movement that, in 2020, launched waves of protests (some peaceful, some violent); the so-called "anti-racism" movement championed by Ibram X. Kendi and others; and the "Defund the Police" movement.

These radical activist movements have their ideological roots sunk into Marxist soil. They all profess a belief that Western society is riddled with "systemic oppression" of women, racial minorities, and gender minorities. The stated goal of these movements is to tear down "hierarchies of power"—but in reality, they are targeting Western civilization (including Christianity) for destruction.

Black Lives Matter's cofounder Patrisse Cullors proudly calls herself and cofounder Alicia Garza "trained Marxists." Cullors was recruited at age 17 by the radical activist Eric Mann (a veteran of Students for a Democratic Society, the Weathermen, and the Black Panther Party). For a decade, Cullors trained to be a radical Marxist organizer.[29]

In the summer of 2020, Black Lives Matter led waves of protests that spread across America. Many protests turned into riots. Rioters defaced monuments, toppled statues, looted stores, and set cars and buildings ablaze. At least 25 people were killed in Black Lives Matter riots.[30] According to Axios, the BLM riots were the "most expensive in insurance history."[31]

By the fall of 2020, Black Lives Matter had deleted the "What We Believe" page from its website after conservative groups took note and began to publicize BLM's true agenda. One of the statements on that page stated that BLM seeks to "disrupt the Western-prescribed nuclear family structure."[32]

This is exactly the sort of goal you would expect from an organization founded by "trained Marxists." Karl Marx, the founder of Communism, stated that one of his main goals was to destroy the family—to completely eliminate families from society. In Chapter 2 of *The Communist Manifesto*, Marx writes:

> Abolition of the family!... [This is the] infamous proposal of the Communists.
>
> On what foundation is the present family, the bourgeois family, based? On capital, on private gain. In its completely developed form, this family exists only among the bourgeoisie. But this state of things finds its complement in the practical absence of the family among the proletarians, and in public prostitution.

> The bourgeois family will vanish...with the vanishing of capital.[33]

Today's radical neo-Marxist activists divide society into oppressors and victims based on race, gender, and other identities. They claim that "white males" are oppressors due to their "systemic privilege," that all "cisgender" and "heteronormative" people oppress the "LGBTQ+" community, that people of a healthy body weight impose "fatphobia" and "body-shaming" on "plus-size" people, that able-bodied people (or "ableists") oppress those with disabilities, and that Christians and Jews oppress people of other religions (or no religion at all). This lexicon relies on a neo-Marxist concept called "intersectionality," which ranks people on a scale depending upon how "privileged" or "oppressed" they are.

It seems clear that Marxism and "woke" neo-Marxism are effective tools that Satan has used to attack Western civilization, undermine Judeo-Christian values, destroy families and individual lives, and plunge vast masses of people into spiritual enslavement and ignorance. Those who would divide us by race, gender, and other identities cling to a set of demonic ideas advanced by one of the most evil men in history, Karl Marx.

According to the authors of the authoritative study *The Black Book of Communism*, "between 85 million and 100 million" people have been murdered by Communist regimes (including the Soviet Union, Communist China, Cambodia under the Khmer Rouge, Vietnam, and North Korea). The authors conclude that "the Communist record offers the most colossal case of political carnage in history."[34]

These murderous regimes are the philosophical allies of radical-left activists who are even now working day and night to tear down our civilization from within.

AN INCREASINGLY CRUEL, CORROSIVE WORLD

The pre-Christian world was a cruel and corrosive world. Slavery was an accepted practice in every society on Earth. Governments maintained order through terror, murder, and torture. In the pre-Christian Roman Empire, crucifixion was commonplace.

At the Battle of the Silarius River in 71 BC, the Roman army under general Marcus Licinius Crassus captured 6,000 rebellious slaves. Crassus ordered that they all be crucified. Imagine 6,000 crosses, each with a dying man nailed to its timbers—a line of crosses 132 miles long, from Rome to Capua. Did this gruesome sight trouble Roman consciences? Not at all. The Romans depended on slavery for their prosperity. The threat of crucifixion kept slaves in their place.

It was into this brutal world that Jesus came, preaching a new message: "You have heard that it was said, 'You shall love your neighbor and hate your enemy.' But I say to you, love your enemies, bless those who curse you, do good to those who hate you, and pray for those who spitefully use you and persecute you, that you may be sons of your Father in heaven" (Matthew 5:43-45 NKJV).

No one had ever heard such a message before. This one man, Jesus of Nazareth, literally changed the world. Today, slavery and torture are officially outlawed throughout Western civilization. Compassion is written into law. There are still brutal societies in the world—but they are societies that have never been impacted by the gospel of Jesus Christ.

But now the world has changed once more. We are living in a post-Christian world, a world that has increasingly rejected the teachings of Jesus. This post-Christian world is now beginning to resemble the pre-Christian world. The further we move from the teachings of Jesus, the more corrosive and violent our world is becoming. Like the ancient Romans, an increasing number of people today embrace the notion that murder is an acceptable way to solve disputes. The thin veneer of civilization is eroding, revealing the barbarism that lurks just beneath the surface.

We saw this barbarism revealed after the 2024 murder of Brian Thompson, the chief executive officer of UnitedHealthcare and a father of two. On December 4, Thompson was in New York for an investors meeting. He left his hotel and walked across the street toward the convention hall. While walking along West 54th Street at 6:45 a.m., a man in a hooded jacket shot him in the back, then shot him again after he fell to the pavement, killing him. A suspect was arrested five days later in Altoona, Pennsylvania, and charged with murder.

It was a horrifying and senseless crime—but not everyone was horrified. In fact, social media exploded with praise for the killer and hatred for the murdered man. One person sneered on TikTok, "Thoughts and deductibles to the family. Unfortunately, my condolences are out-of-network." Another posted, "This needs to be the new norm. EAT THE RICH."[35]

One US Senator—a longtime critic of the healthcare industry—expressed what sounded like sympathy for the killer and those who praised him: "The visceral response from people across this country who feel cheated, ripped off, and threatened by the vile practices of their insurance companies should be a warning to everyone in the health care system. Violence is never the answer, but people can be pushed only so far."[36]

A poll conducted a few days later by Emerson College Polling found that 41 percent of adults under age 30 viewed the cold-blooded killing of the healthcare executive as—are you ready for this?—"acceptable."[37]

In pre-Christian Rome, people rationalized slavery and approved of crucifixion. In post-Christian America, people increasingly rationalize murder as a solution to political and economic disputes. And echoing in the background of these chilling opinion polls, we can hear the gloating laughter of demons.

AN ANCIENT, ONGOING, INVISIBLE WAR

A nonbeliever might look at these events and say, "What's wrong with people? What is this world coming to? Are people losing their minds?"

But spiritually insightful believers look at these events and say, "Satan's up to his old tricks. He's using the same old strategies and deceptions he used against Adam and Eve—and they're still working! Oh, he dresses them up in nice modern disguises so they appear new to undiscerning people. He can misdirect the directionless—but he can't fool the wise. Everything that's happening is part of the invisible war that has been raging since the beginning of time."

This invisible war was raging in the first-century world. The early church was on the front lines of that war. There is a scene in Acts 20 where the apostle Paul speaks to the leaders of the church in Ephesus. Just before Paul leaves Ephesus to return to Jerusalem, he warns them of the battles they will face in the invisible war:

> Keep watch over yourselves and all the flock of which the Holy Spirit has made you overseers. Be shepherds of the church of God, which he bought with his own blood. I know that after I leave, savage wolves will come in among you and will not spare the flock. Even from your own number men will arise and distort the truth in order to draw away disciples after them. So be on your guard! (Acts 20:28-31).

I have been to the ruins of Ephesus on the Ionian coast, southwest of Selçuk in İzmir Province, Turkey. Ephesus was famed for its grand architecture—the Temple of Artemis, the Library of Celsus, and the great open-air theater. It was a moving experience to stand on that historic ground, in the stillness of those broken and time-worn columns.

I imagined Paul's commanding voice, urging those church leaders to be inwardly vigilant and outwardly attentive to the needs of God's flock, to be true shepherds of God's church. In my mind, I could hear Paul warning them that, from within the church itself, maybe even from among those leaders, savage wolves would arise to draw people away from the truth.

Paul reminded the Ephesian leaders of a principle that many preachers and teachers seem to forget in these days: It is not our church! It is not the church of this pastor or that teacher. It is the church of Jesus Christ, which he purchased with his blood.

Paul's words of encouragement and warning to those church leaders still echo with urgency in our world today. The invisible war still rages all around us and within us. The "savage wolves" Paul warns about continue to attack the church of Jesus Christ today. Tragically, the wolves sometimes win. Over the decades, I have seen individual Christians and entire churches fall as casualties in the invisible war.

OUR CUNNING AND RUTHLESS ADVERSARY

In order to win the invisible war, we need to understand the commanding general of the opposing army. We need to understand the enemy of our souls, the enemy of the church.

Satan is not wise, but he is incredibly intelligent—and we should never underestimate him. He's cunning, he's conniving, he's deceptive. He is a master of subterfuge and infiltration. He knows how to worm his way into the church and use church people to achieve his goals. He's absolutely ruthless in his campaign to destroy the church Jesus has built.

But please don't let Satan frighten you. In fact, the central theme of this book is that we should be bold and courageous as we fight our spiritual battles. In the coming chapters, I'll give you the tools to be victorious in our war against Satan. I will show you again and again that the Lord who is in us, the Lord who leads us, is greater than Satan. Victory is a matter of knowing how to lay hold of God's power for the battles of this life.

Can Satan really deceive people in the church? Can he delude and destroy a congregation or an individual Christian? Yes, it has happened again and again through the centuries. There have been in the past—and there will be in the future—tragic casualties of the invisible war.

But Satan can *never* defeat the church of Jesus Christ, the body of believers, the elect of God from every tongue, tribe, and nation. Satan can never destroy the church as a whole. Jesus has promised that the gates of hell cannot prevail against his church. He will lead us to a complete and ultimate victory.

My goal in this book is to arm you so that you will be a victor in this war—not a victim of Satan's deceptive strategies.

In these days—and we are seeing increasing signs that these may really be the last days—it seems that the remnant of faithful believers is diminishing. More and more people in the church are falling away from a faith in the uncompromised Word of God. I believe this is because increasing numbers of professing Christians are falling prey to Satan's strategies.

But even though the faithful remnant is dwindling, I am not discouraged. Numbers don't matter. After all, Jesus used 12 men to turn the world upside down and build his church. We choose to be aware of Satan's strategies and advance God's kingdom in the world.

As you are about to see, Satan is already defeated. Though it may not always seem like it, we have already won the invisible war.

2

THE BATTLE WITHIN

Whether in military campaigns or spiritual struggles, decisive commitment is essential. The old saying is true: "He who hesitates is lost." We must persevere until the victory is won. And we must commit ourselves fully to the lordship and leadership of our Commander, Jesus Christ.

THE BATTLE WITHIN

In 1861, after the Union defeat at the First Battle of Bull Run, President Abraham Lincoln appointed General George B. McClellan as commander of the Army of the Potomac. It was a decision President Lincoln would soon regret.

Famed for his organizational skills, McClellan turned the Army of the Potomac into a disciplined force. But when he led that force onto the battlefield—

He hesitated.

Again and again, McClellan would have all the advantages in his favor—numerical superiority, advantageous terrain, good weather—yet he would not attack the enemy. McClellan's half-hearted approach to war baffled and frustrated Lincoln. Finally, he sent McClellan a telegram that read, "If General McClellan does not want to use the Army, I would like to borrow it for a time, provided I could see how it could be made to do something."[1]

Lincoln's dissatisfaction grew during the Peninsular Campaign of 1862. McClellan, believing the Confederates had far more troops than they did, advanced cautiously toward Richmond. His delay allowed the beleaguered Confederates time to regroup and mount an effective counterattack.

McClellan had squandered the Union's early advantages, allowing the Confederates to seize the initiative. Decisive action might have turned the tide—but McClellan's lukewarm approach prolonged the war and led to more casualties on both sides.

Lincoln eventually replaced McClellan with General Ambrose Burnside, a flawed but aggressive battlefield leader. Only when strong, decisive generals like Burnside and Ulysses S. Grant took control did the Civil War begin to tilt in favor of the Union.[2]

From my reading of history, I'm convinced that a key principle of both military warfare and spiritual warfare is this: *Half-heartedness is more harmful to our cause than retreat.* A half-hearted approach to the battle increases the odds of defeat by wasting opportunities and emboldening the enemy. You can always retreat to regroup for a future offensive. But half-hearted efforts lead to stalemates and destroyed lives.

Whether in military campaigns or spiritual struggles, decisive commitment is essential. The old saying is true: "He who hesitates is lost." We must persevere until the victory is won. And we must commit ourselves fully to the lordship and leadership of our Commander, Jesus Christ.

THE DOORS OF YOUR SOUL

Some people think that being a Christian means that you commit your life to Jesus Christ as your Lord and Savior—and that's it! You're in. You've checked the box. Mission accomplished.

But surrendering to Jesus is only the first step of a long journey. It's an important step. It's a decisive step. By acknowledging that there is no other way to salvation except through Jesus, you have moved from darkness to light. You've changed your destination from hell to heaven, but—

You are still a long way from finishing your journey. You are not yet sanctified—far from it.

Let me put it this way: When you come to Christ, you are like a massive corporation that has just been sold to a new owner. Though you are under new ownership, the old management structure is still in place. The old ways of doing things still prevail. It will take time for the new owner to impose his will on the corporation, install new practices, root out the deadwood and the mischief-makers, and remake the corporation into his image.

Or let me suggest another analogy: Your spiritual life is like a house with many doors. Each door opens into your soul. Each door needs to be bolted securely to prevent illegal entry by thieves and marauders. But the process of bolting all of those doors takes time. They have to be shut and bolted one by one.

The act of identifying and securing each of those doors is called sanctification. It's the process of finding all the sins, attitudes, bad habits, and character flaws in your life that leave you vulnerable to invasion and infiltration by the enemy. The goal of sanctification is to securely fasten every door of your life so that Satan's foot soldiers can't find their way in.

In the Middle East, the region where I was born, thieves are very gentlemanlike. They seldom steal during the day. They never break down doors and crash into your house. No, they wait until nighttime, when it's dark and quiet. They go to shops and homes—and they are careful not to make a sound. They don't want to disturb your sleep or wake your neighbors.

They go up to a door and press their hand lightly against it—just in case the homeowner or shopkeeper has forgotten to lock the door. If the door opens, then they walk in on tiptoes, quietly steal what they want, and then leave as quietly as they came.

Satan, too, is a gentleman thief. He quietly approaches the doors of your life and applies gentle pressure—just a slight push to see if the door is unlocked. If you have not secured that door of your life, Satan will come in and help himself.

So I urge you to beware of the unlocked doors in your life. Don't assume that because you once made a decision for Christ a few days or months or years ago, you have accomplished God's mission for your life. No matter how long you have been a Christian, you can be certain that God is calling you onward. He wants to reveal to you the doors of your life that are still unlocked, that still leave you vulnerable to Satan's attacks.

What would an unlocked door of your life look like? It might be unresolved anger and resentment. There might be someone in your life who has hurt you, and you have not forgiven that hurt. Or you might have a habit of lying or cutting ethical corners. Or you might have an addiction to alcohol or tobacco or drugs or pornography. Or you might have a habit of filthy language. Or you might envy the possessions of your neighbor. Or you might have a habit of lustful thoughts. Or you might be obsessed with greed and thoughts of discontentment.

This is not a complete list of possible unlocked doors—far from it. I only listed a very few common possibilities—and the Lord may bring many other unlocked doors to your mind. And please understand, most of these doors have to be bolted again and again. You can't lock them once and assume they will stay that way. You have to be continuously on guard. You need to bolt and re-bolt and re-re-bolt the doors of your life to make sure you are not granting the enemy access to your soul.

Now, I don't want you to worry and think, *Oh, this is going to be hard work! There's going to be so much to remember, so many doors to bolt. I don't think I can do this!* No, living the sanctified Christian life is *not* a life of perpetual worry and insecurity.

Gaining the victory in this invisible war is not a lot of hard work and rules to remember. It's actually quite simple because the hard work has already been done—by Jesus.

The outcome of the invisible war is already decided. The victory is won. The enemy is defeated. We are the only army in history that is granted success before firing a shot. Yes, there will be clashes and skirmishes. These battles can be costly to the unwary—but the final outcome is never in doubt.

Shortly before he went to the cross, Jesus said, "Now is the time for judgment on this world; now the prince of this world will be driven out" (John 12:31). The victory was won on the cross of Calvary.

SATAN'S BATTLE MANUAL

To win any war, military or spiritual, you must have the will to win, and you must know your enemy. The best way to know your enemy is to read his battle manual. And Satan's battle manual is right out in the open, waiting for us to read it. His strategy is not a secret. It's there for all to see.

In sports, most coaches guard their playbook with their lives. They don't want to give their opponents any advantages. But Satan's battle manual is easy to find, easy to read—yet very hard to defeat. In fact, it is impossible to defeat Satan's strategies without the power of God through complete surrender to Jesus.

You need to know how Satan attacks, when he attacks, and where he attacks. You need to be in a constant state of readiness. Then, when you know exactly how Satan's attack will take place, you need to build up your defenses and your armor against that attack. I know this from personal experience.

When I prepare to write or speak on a certain topic or a passage of Scripture, I know I need to prepare myself spiritually. I not only need to study the Scriptures so that I can prepare my message. I need to *prepare myself*—personally, spiritually, and mentally, so that Satan can't ambush me on that particular subject.

From time to time I sense God calling me to talk about some

aspect of the invisible war—about the strategies of our enemy, about the need to be fully surrendered to Jesus, about the need to cling to God's Word and put on the full armor of God. And the moment I decide it's time to give that talk, I know I'm in for days and weeks of relentless spiritual attack. I will face attacks in my circumstances and attacks in my relationships. Most of all, I will experience attacks in my spirit and in my emotions. These attacks are indescribable, and they are dark.

Yet the Holy Spirit comes to me in those moments and makes me aware that I'm not just feeling down, I'm not just feeling blue. He lets me know that *I am under attack*. And as the Spirit brings light to my understanding, I regain my spiritual balance and my joy.

MAKE SATAN AFRAID OF YOU

Always remember that, if you are in Christ Jesus, you are on the winning side. And when you are on the winning side, you have nothing to fear.

Does it surprise you to learn that you don't have to be afraid of Satan? While it's true that Satan is the enemy of your soul, you truly have nothing to fear from him. You must never be afraid of Satan—*never*.

In fact, your mission as a follower of Christ is to *make Satan afraid of you*. As James the apostle wrote, "Submit yourselves, then, to God. Resist the devil, and he will flee from you" (James 4:7). What have you done lately to scare the devil? What victory have you scored to make him run for cover?

The First Great Awakening was a wave of evangelical revivals that swept through Britain and the Thirteen American Colonies in the 1730s and 1740s. One of the leading evangelists of the First Great Awakening was the English preacher George Whitefield. There were also opponents of the wave of revivals, including a Congregational clergyman, Charles Chauncy of Boston. He was an early advocate of Unitarianism—a set of beliefs that rejected the deity of Jesus, the doctrine of the Trinity, and the finality of God's judgment.

When George Whitefield sailed from England to Boston to hold a series of evangelistic meetings, he happened to encounter Charles Chauncy on the street.

Chauncy frowned and said, "I'm sorry to see you here again, Mr. Whitefield."

Whitefield smiled. "And so is the devil," he said.[3]

Tens of thousands of people came to Christ in New England as a result of George Whitefield's preaching. That's why Satan was afraid of George Whitefield.

We must ask ourselves: Is Satan afraid of us? And if not, why not?

One reason Satan does not fear some professing Christians is that they do not believe that the whole Bible is the Word of God. They call Genesis a myth and Revelation a mystery. I don't believe human beings are clever enough to devise this formula. I believe the notion that Genesis is a myth and Revelation is a mystery was inspired by the devil himself. Why? Because the devil is eager to get rid of both of these books.

In Genesis, God pronounces sentence against the devil: "I will put enmity between you and the woman, and between your offspring and hers; he will crush your head, and you will strike his heel" (Genesis 3:15). In Revelation, God executes the sentence against the devil: "The devil, who deceived them, was thrown into the lake of burning sulfur, where the beast and the false prophet had been thrown. They will be tormented day and night for ever and ever" (Revelation 20:10).

Satan hates both of those books—the first and the last, Genesis and Revelation—and it's easy to see why he hates them. That is why Satan has planted slanders about these books in the minds of many professing Christians.

SATAN: A SELF-DECEIVED DECEIVER

Satan is a deceiver. Who is the greatest victim of his deception? Satan himself! He believes his own lies. He hates to be reminded of his imminent destruction. He tries to convince himself it won't happen. That's why he is working overtime all around the globe, preparing the human race to welcome the Antichrist. He knows the time is drawing near when he will be thrown into "the lake of burning sulfur."

I can guarantee that the devil does not want you to read to the end of this book. You may notice that distractions and interruptions pop into your life, drawing you away from this book. Why? Because Satan knows that, in these pages, you are going to be blessed with the tools for victory over him. So he will do everything in his power to keep you from reading, to keep you from becoming aware of his tactics.

I'm often asked: Where did Satan come from? That is an important question. There are two passages in the Bible that tell us exactly where the devil came from. The first is from the book of Isaiah:

> How you have fallen from heaven,
>   morning star, son of the dawn!
> You have been cast down to the earth,
>   you who once laid low the nations!
> You said in your heart,
>   "I will ascend to the heavens;
> I will raise my throne
>   above the stars of God;
> I will sit enthroned on the mount of assembly,
>   on the utmost heights of Mount Zaphon.
> I will ascend above the tops of the clouds;
>   I will make myself like the Most High."

> But you are brought down to the realm of the dead,
> to the depths of the pit (Isaiah 14:12-15).

Where the NIV translation reads, "How you have fallen from heaven, morning star, son of the dawn," the New King James Version reads, "How you are fallen from heaven, O Lucifer, son of the morning!" The original Hebrew word that is translated either "morning star" or "O Lucifer" is *hêlēl*. It appears in only this one verse in the entire Old Testament, and it can mean "light-bearer" or "shining one" or "morning star."

The word *Lucifer* comes from the Latin Vulgate translation of Isaiah 14:12, which translates *hêlēl* as *lucifer* (meaning "light-bearer" in Latin). This is one of the great paradoxes of Scripture, the fact that the most evil and destructive figure in the Bible was literally the shining light-bearer of heaven before his rebellion and fall.

The second passage that describes the origin of the devil is from the book of Ezekiel:

> You were the seal of perfection,
> full of wisdom and perfect in beauty.
> You were in Eden,
> the garden of God;
> every precious stone adorned you:
> carnelian, chrysolite and emerald,
> topaz, onyx and jasper,
> lapis lazuli, turquoise and beryl.
> Your settings and mountings were made of gold;
> on the day you were created they were prepared.
> You were anointed as a guardian cherub,
> for so I ordained you.
> You were on the holy mount of God;
> you walked among the fiery stones.

> You were blameless in your ways
>   from the day you were created
>   till wickedness was found in you.
> Through your widespread trade
>   you were filled with violence,
>   and you sinned.
> So I drove you in disgrace from the mount of God,
>   and I expelled you, guardian cherub,
>   from among the fiery stones.
> Your heart became proud
>   on account of your beauty,
> and you corrupted your wisdom
>   because of your splendor.
> So I threw you to the earth;
>   I made a spectacle of you before kings.
> By your many sins and dishonest trade
>   you have desecrated your sanctuaries.
> So I made a fire come out from you,
>   and it consumed you,
> and I reduced you to ashes on the ground
>   in the sight of all who were watching.
> All the nations who knew you
>   are appalled at you;
> you have come to a horrible end
>   and will be no more (Ezekiel 28:12-19).

The prophet Ezekiel addresses Satan, saying, "You were the seal of perfection, full of wisdom and perfect in beauty." He is called by many names—Satan, Lucifer, the devil—and he was one of the principal servants of the Lord God in heaven. As verse 14 says, "You were anointed as a guardian cherub."

LUCIFER, THE LIGHT-BEARER

It's important to remember that the light of Lucifer was a *reflected* light. He did not shine with any light of his own. When Isaiah calls him *hêlēl* in Hebrew ("light-bearer" or "shining one" or "morning star"), he is using a word that the Hebrews used to refer to the planet Venus, the "morning star." This is an especially appropriate symbol for Satan, because Venus is not a star. The light that shines from the planet Venus is reflected sunlight.

Just as Venus does not give off any light of its own, Lucifer did not shine with his own light. He bore the reflected light of God.

Lucifer served God in the highest level of heaven. While Moses had to cover his face in the presence of God, Lucifer didn't. Lucifer was able to look directly upon the throne of God. He was able to offer praise and worship in God's very presence.

Because Lucifer was a powerful and high-ranking angel of heaven, he is truly a powerful and dangerous adversary as a fallen angel. We dare not try to defeat him in our own strength and wisdom. He's been around for a long, long time, and he knows all the tricks. But you can defeat him by the authority of Jesus in the power of the Holy Spirit.

The rebellion of Satan might be compared to the Director of the US Central Intelligence Agency defecting to the Communists. He knows all the protocols, all the codes, all the agents' names, all the vital secrets of the government. Satan had that kind of high-level position in heaven—and now he not only *works for* the enemy, but he *is* the enemy.

That's why Paul writes, "Satan himself masquerades as an angel of light" (2 Corinthians 11:14). Satan *was* an angel of light—but he is not a light-bearer anymore. So he goes about in disguise. He *masquerades* as an angel of light. He knows how to fool the unwary. He knows how to make evil appear good and good appear evil.

Paul goes on to say, "It is not surprising, then, if his servants also masquerade as servants of righteousness. Their end will be what their actions deserve" (2 Corinthians 11:15). There are many people, both outside of the church and within the church, who serve Satan. Some are evil people who knowingly do evil. Others are simply unwise and gullible, and they have bought into Satan's lies. Whether knowingly or unwittingly, Satan's servants masquerade as servants of righteousness.

THE REBELLION AND FALL OF LUCIFER

What happened to Lucifer? Why did he rebel against God and fall from heaven?

Remember that Lucifer was beautiful and wise. God had entrusted Lucifer with enormous, delegated authority. This means that Lucifer commanded many angels in accordance with the authority God had vested in him. How many angels did Lucifer oversee? We don't know—but given the vastness of our universe, the number could easily have been in the billions or trillions.

When Lucifer in his arrogance rebelled against God, he led one-third of the angels of heaven in an attempted *coup d'état*. Lucifer wanted to unseat God and take God's place on the heavenly throne so that he could receive the worship that is rightfully God's. Lucifer wanted to be worshipped then—and he still seeks to be worshipped now.

One-third of the angels followed Lucifer in his self-destructive folly. How do we know this? We find these words in the book of Revelation: "Then another sign appeared in heaven: an enormous red dragon with seven heads and ten horns and seven crowns on its heads. Its tail swept a third of the stars out of the sky and flung them to the earth" (Revelation 12:3-4). This is a symbolic depiction of Lucifer's rebellion against God—and the stars that the dragon's tail sweeps from the sky and flings to Earth are his rebellious angels.

How did Lucifer persuade one-third of the angels of heaven to join in his rebellion? I believe Lucifer offered them incentives, just as he offers you and me incentives to disobey God. He probably offered them the equivalent of promotions and bonuses, much as a corporate executive might offer an important job candidate the use of the company jet and trips to a ski resort. Each rebellious angel was probably offered rewards in keeping with his rank.

This is Satan's recruitment strategy. He uses the same kinds of incentives to get you and me to disobey God and join his unholy cause. Satan's modus operandi is to offer you the world and pay you with trash. He promises the best and pays out the worst. He promises you pleasure and pays you with pain. He promises you profits and pays you with losses. He promises you life and pays you with death. His methods haven't changed since time began. He deceived a third of the heavenly host, and he continues to deceive humanity on Earth.

If you compare heaven to a corporation, you might say that Lucifer was the Chief Operating Officer (COO), administering the "corporation" under the executive leadership of God, the Chief Executive Officer (CEO). In the corporate world, it's reasonable for the COO to seek a promotion when the CEO retires. The problem with Lucifer's ambition was that the CEO—God—was never going to retire. In the heavenly realm, there is an unbridgeable gulf between the Creator and his creation, including his angels.

But Lucifer's ego was boundless and unstoppable. He wanted to unseat God and take his place. The prophet Isaiah said of Lucifer, "You said in your heart, 'I will ascend to the heavens; I will raise my throne above the stars of God; I will sit enthroned on the mount of assembly'" (Isaiah 14:13). Notice that repeated phrase: "I will…I will…I will." In his arrogance, Lucifer chose to exalt his will above God's will. He was so proud of his beauty, intellect, and attainment that he failed to recognize that everything he had was from God. Without God he was nothing.

The Lord Jesus Christ, the Son of God, the second Person of the

Trinity, was there before the beginning of time. Paul writes of Jesus, "In him all things were created: things in heaven and on earth, visible and invisible, whether thrones or powers or rulers or authorities; all things have been created through him and for him" (Colossians 1:16). So Jesus was there when Satan led his rebellion against God. That is why Jesus told his followers, "I saw Satan fall like lightning from heaven" (Luke 10:18).

THREE TROUBLING QUESTIONS

There are three questions that people always ask about Satan's rebellion:

First question: Did God know from the beginning that pride would capture Lucifer's heart? Answer: Yes, he knew. God is omniscient, which means that he knows everything ahead of time.

Second question: Could God have prevented Lucifer from falling into pride and rebellion? Answer: Yes, God is omnipotent. He has the power to do anything, including preventing Satan from committing sin.

Third question: If God knew what Lucifer would do *and* if God could have prevented Lucifer from doing it, why didn't he? That is a question that has kept philosophers and theologians awake at night.

I'm sure every believer ponders that question at one time or another, thinking, *If God had only prevented the fall of Satan, he would have saved the entire human race so much pain and heartache! He would have saved me pain and heartache! There would have been no fall of Adam and Eve. There would have been no history of human sin. There would have been no need for Jesus to die on the cross to redeem us from death and sin.*

Yes, God could have created robots to serve in heaven, and he could have placed a pair of robots in the Garden of Eden. But God didn't want either angels or human beings to be robots. He wanted to create beings who possessed moral free will. He wanted to create beings with the ability to *choose* to love and obey God.

But it is simply a logical fact that God cannot create beings who are free to love him and obey him unless those beings are also free to reject him and rebel against him. There is no free will without the freedom to make bad choices. Obedience and devotion can only exist when they are given freely.

God is not a puppet master. He is our Father and Redeemer. He wants to have a genuine relationship with us—a relationship in which we willingly *choose* to love and obey him. Lucifer's fall was a necessary part of God's larger plan involving the redemption and salvation of the human race. As the apostle John tells us, "The devil has been sinning from the beginning. The reason the Son of God appeared was to destroy the devil's work" (1 John 3:8).

While it's tempting to think we would be better off if Satan had never rebelled and fallen, we have to recognize we don't really know that. We can't claim to be wiser than God. We can't claim to understand his plans and purposes. The moment we begin to think we could do a better job of managing heaven and Earth, we have fallen into the same sin by which Satan and his angels fell.

DON'T FALL FOR LUCIFER'S SIN

The sin of Lucifer has been repeated again and again through the centuries. It was repeated by Adam and Eve, who believed the serpent's lie and wanted to be like God, knowing good and evil. It was repeated by Israel when they entered the Promised Land and began to worship and sacrifice to Baal instead of the God who had redeemed them from slavery in Egypt. The sin of Lucifer was repeated by the Pharisees who rejected and plotted to kill their anointed Messiah, the Lord Jesus Christ. It is repeated today by everyone who rejects Jesus and his salvation.

But the most tragic sin of all is when Christians repeat the sin of Lucifer, when they fall for his lies, when they fall prey to the satanic sin of pride. The sin of pride destroys your judgment. It makes you feel entitled to things you have no right to have. It alienates you from God.

People sometimes ask, "Michael, do you ever struggle with pride?" I say, "Are you kidding me? More than you'll ever know!" Pride is a daily, even moment-by-moment battle in my life. I fear my own pride because I have seen so many Christian leaders toppled by pride. I am very sober minded when I ponder the warning of the apostle Paul: "Do not think of yourself more highly than you ought" (Romans 12:3).

The sin of pride is one of those doors in the house of our souls. Leave that door open just a crack, and Satan will come bounding into your life, wreaking more havoc than you can imagine. I urge you to examine yourself, honestly and soberly, and ask God to point out to you any areas of pride in your life. Hand your pride over to God, not just once, but again and again throughout the day. Keep the door of pride locked and bolted tightly shut. Don't let Satan, the prideful one, gain entrance to your life through the sin of pride.

We have looked at the origin and nature of Satan and his forces, and we have seen how they can gain access to our lives through the "unlocked doors" of our sins, attitudes, and habits. Next, we will look at the struggle between God and his angels versus Satan's forces in our world and in our lives.

3

ANGELS AND DEMONS

God's Word instructs us and reminds us of the unseen battles that rage all around us: "He will command his angels concerning you to guard you in all your ways" (Psalm 91:11). Those words thrill and amaze me. I was born a nobody— yet God assigns mighty angels to look after me. Can you imagine a more exhilarating thought than that? Angels stand watch around my home. They sit next to me when I drive. They steer me around the traps the enemy sets for me.

ANGELS AND DEMONS

A good friend of mine, C. Peter Wagner, was a missionary and a seminary professor. In his book *Prayer Shield*, he tells a story that was told to him by missionary researcher John Vaughn. In the 1970s, while Vaughn was flying from Detroit to Boston, he noticed that the man seated next to him had bowed his head and seemed to be praying.

Vaughn asked him, "Are you a Christian?"

The man seemed surprised by the question. "Oh, no," he said. "I'm not a Christian. I'm actually a Satanist."

This wasn't the answer Vaughn expected. He asked the man what he was praying for.

The man replied, "My primary attention is directed toward the fall of Christian pastors and their families living in New England." Then he asked Vaughn what he was planning to do in Boston.

Vaughn said he was going to speak at a seminar for Christian pastors. His goal was to prepare pastors to better serve the kingdom of God.

The man didn't want to hear any more—so he bowed his head and continued praying to Satan.

Pete Wagner concluded, "This encounter made John realize just how essential intercession for pastors really is…Whose prayer was answered—the Christian's or the satanist's?"[1]

Why would Satan target pastors for failure? It's because Satan knows the importance of a command structure. Some of the old hymns of the church acknowledge that the church is engaged in battle—hymns like "Onward Christian Soldiers," "Am I a Soldier of the Cross?," and "A Mighty Fortress Is Our God," to name a few. Unfortunately, that perspective of the church's role as an army against evil has been abandoned in many corners of Christianity.

But the Scriptures make it clear that God designed the church to be a fighting force, taking territory for the kingdom, fully engaged in spiritual warfare. This means that the church is structured like an army, with leaders and strategists who give direction to the troops. Satan knows that if he can destroy those leaders and strategists, he can cripple the ability of the church to prevail in the invisible war.

Satan understands the importance of a command structure because he himself operates with a command structure. The demonic hierarchy resembles the angelic hierarchy in heaven.

DEMONS IN THE PUBLIC SQUARE

Whether we like it or not, Satan is at war with each of us. He is viciously cruel, and he does not fight fairly. In the 1970s, when John Vaughn encountered a Satanist praying quietly on a flight to Boston, Satanists operated in secret. Today, Satanists are out in the open, setting up in-your-face demonic displays in the public square. Here are a few examples:

In Iowa in 2024, the local Satanic Temple hosted a public reading marathon on the Tama County Courthouse lawn. Over two days, Satanists read from *Paradise Lost* (the 1667 epic poem by John Milton about Satan's temptation of Adam and Eve) and *The Revolt of the Angels* by Anatole France (about Satan's rebellion against God). The

Satanic Temple sponsored this event in response to such Christian events as the Iowa 99 County Bible Reading Marathon.²

Also in 2024, the legislatures of Oklahoma and Florida passed laws allowing ministers, rabbis, priests, imams, and laypeople—if they meet certain qualifications and pass a background check—to volunteer as chaplains at public schools. These chaplains attempt to meet the needs of students when school counselors are in short supply—and because volunteers can be Christian, Jewish, or Islamic, these laws do not violate the establishment clause of the First Amendment.

In response, leaders of the Satanic Temple have vowed to flood public schools with Satanic volunteer "counselors." Of course, these Satanic "counselors" don't want to help students cope with crises. They have clearly stated that they want to shut down the chaplain programs in these states.³

At Christmastime in 2024, the Satanic Temple placed Satanic displays at state government buildings in several states (including Minnesota, New Hampshire, and Vermont). Satanic symbols appeared prominently alongside Christmas trees, Nativity scenes, and Hanukkah menorahs.

The Satanic display in New Hampshire's capital city of Concord included a statue of Baphomet, a demonic idol with a goat-like head and yellow eyes, clad in a black cloak with occult symbols, standing beside a tablet inscribed with the Satanic Temple's seven tenets. The Satanists declared that they "champion the symbol of Lucifer as one of revolt against arbitrary authority and advocacy for the pursuit of knowledge."

In a statement on Facebook, the city of Concord said it allowed the Satanic display in order to avoid being sued. "Throughout the country," the statement said, "the Satanic Temple has both threatened and brought lawsuits under the First Amendment when excluded."⁴

GOD'S ARMY VS. SATAN'S ARMY

People sometimes say of a sleeping child, "Oh, isn't he a little angel?" Many people view angels as adorable, childlike creatures. Greeting card portrayals of angels often make them seem ethereal and even effeminate. The biblical reality of angels is very different from the popular stereotypes.

An angel is a fearsome creature. If an angel appeared to you right now, you might suffer a heart attack. In the Bible, whenever angels appear to people—whether to Hagar in the Old Testament or Joseph, Mary, or the women at Jesus's tomb in the New Testament—they always have to calm people down with the words, "Don't be afraid!" (See Genesis 21:17; Matthew 1:20, 28:5; Luke 1:13, 1:30, 2:10.) God's holy angels are truly terrifying creatures.

When you think of angels, you should forget about greeting card images. Instead, think of angels as God's Delta Force, Navy SEALs, Army Rangers, and Green Berets. Angels have a command structure—and Satan has copied that command structure. Let's take a closer look at five aspects of the angelic hosts so that we can better understand the nature of the invisible war that rages around us.

First: Some of the leaders in the angelic chain of command are named in the Bible. There is Michael the Archangel, mentioned in Jude 1:9; Daniel 10:13, 21; and Revelation 12:7-8. The angel Gabriel is mentioned in Daniel 8:16 and 9:21, and twice in Luke 1. The only other angels mentioned by name are the fallen angels Lucifer (or Satan) and Abaddon (or Apollyon), the "the angel of the Abyss" in Revelation 9:11.

Angels have individual personalities. They have a powerful intellect, real feelings, and free will. That's why a third of the angels of heaven rebelled and chose to follow Satan. Angels also have individual functions as they carry out the will of God. The loyal angels of heaven implement the plan of God in the lives of those who have submitted themselves to the lordship of Jesus Christ.

Second: Angels live forever. Gabriel appeared to the prophet Daniel in Daniel 10. Then, four centuries later, Gabriel appeared twice in Luke 1, first to the godly priest Zechariah and then to the virgin Mary. Angels are not bound by time. The angelic host cannot be depleted by death.

Many people have the mistaken notion that when we die, we become angels. This misconception may be the result of a misinterpretation of the words of Jesus: "At the resurrection people will neither marry nor be given in marriage; they will be like the angels in heaven" (Matthew 22:30). But Jesus never said that we would *become* angels, only that we would be *like* the angels in the sense that we will not have physical limitations. In heaven, we will live forever, as the angels do.

THE FORM OF ANGELS

Third: Angels have bodies. Their bodies are not like our bodies, but they do have a physical form. Daniel said, "There before me stood one who looked like a man" (Daniel 8:15). He said that the angel Gabriel had the appearance of a man, but he was clearly not a man. Angel bodies are totally unlike our bodies. Angel bodies are designed by a different set of rules, and they function in different realms. But they do have a recognizable likeness and similarity to human form.

When we are resurrected, our bodies will not be angel bodies but will be like the resurrected body of Jesus. We will not be limited by time and space, and we will not be subject to hunger, exhaustion, sickness, or death. The Gospels tell us that Jesus was seen in Galilee and in Jerusalem soon after the resurrection and shortly before the Ascension. Galilee and Jerusalem are about 120 miles apart—several days' journey on foot. So it seems clear that time and space did not hinder the travels of the post-resurrection Jesus. He could undoubtedly appear wherever he wanted at the speed of thought.

Fourth: Angels were created first. They were created before the heavens and the earth were created, and before humanity existed. As God told Job:

> Where were you when I laid the earth's foundation?
> Tell me, if you understand.
> Who marked off its dimensions? Surely you know!
> Who stretched a measuring line across it?
> On what were its footings set,
> or who laid its cornerstone—
> while the morning stars sang together
> and all the angels shouted for joy? (Job 38:4-7).

Did you notice the chronology of events in that passage? God tells Job that "all the angels shouted for joy" as they watched God laying the foundation of the earth. The angels existed before the beginning of creation.

Paul tells us, "The Son is the image of the invisible God, the firstborn over all creation. For in him all things were created: things in heaven and on earth, visible and invisible, whether thrones or powers or rulers or authorities; all things have been created through him and for him" (Colossians 1:15-16). Notice that through Jesus the Son everything was created, both "visible and invisible."

Many people today say that if a thing cannot be experienced by the senses or measured by scientific instruments, it doesn't exist. All who say such things will be put to shame when God unveils the invisible world for the human race to see.

In this verse, Paul defines the angelic hierarchy: *Thrones* are at the top of the angelic command structure. *Powers* (or dominions) rank second. *Rulers* (or principalities) rank third. And *authorities* rank fourth—these are the angelic foot soldiers who come to minister and protect believers from harm.

(By the way, I want to avoid any confusion about these terms in case you are following a different translation. The New International Version lists this hierarchy as "thrones or powers or rulers or authorities." The King James Version and the American Standard Version list this hierarchy as "thrones, or dominions, or principalities, or powers." The New American Standard Bible lists the hierarchy as "thrones, or dominions, or rulers, or authorities." The specific English words used here are not as important as the concept that Paul is conveying, which is that there are levels or ranks within the hierarchy of the angels of heaven.)

At the top of the hierarchy, Paul lists "thrones." In the hierarchy of heaven, there is one throne, the throne of God. Every level of the hierarchy beneath the throne exists to execute God's will and administer his universe. How many angels occupy these other levels? Too many to count. That's why many biblical passages call God "the Lord of hosts."[5]

When Jesus was arrested before the crucifixion, he told his disciples, "Do you think I cannot call on my Father, and he will at once put at my disposal more than twelve legions of angels?" (Matthew 26:53). He was comparing the angels of heaven to Roman legions, which consisted of about 6,000 soldiers each. Twelve legions of angels would total 72,000 angels.

Our God is the God of power and might. He commands vast armies of angelic forces. He is a God of order, and he ranks them according to a chain of command. Whenever you see disorder and chaos, you know Satan is behind it. Satan is an anarchist who opposes the orderly creation God has made.

THE MISSION OF ANGELS

Fifth: Angels have a specific task to carry out. No two angels are exactly alike—and none with identical jobs. Each angel has a unique mission to perform. We know this from the story Jesus told of Lazarus and the rich man: "The time came when the beggar died, and the angels carried him to Abraham's side. The rich man also died and was buried" (Luke 16:22). There are angels whose mission is to carry us into the presence of Jesus in glory—but for those who die apart from Jesus, there are no angels, only the grave.

Every moment of every day, there are unseen battles being fought all around us in the invisible war. Satan wants to keep us ignorant of the heavenly realm, of God, and of Satan's attacks. Satan doesn't want us to know about the invisible war.

But God's Word instructs us and reminds us of the unseen battles that rage all around us: "He will command his angels concerning you to guard you in all your ways" (Psalm 91:11). Those words thrill and amaze me. I was born a nobody—yet God assigns mighty angels to look after me. Can you imagine a more exhilarating thought than that? Angels stand watch around my home. They sit next to me when I drive. They steer me around the traps the enemy sets for me.

As we examine the Scriptures, we see examples of God working through angels. I believe God deliberately included these accounts so that we would be encouraged and comforted. He wanted us to live our lives in the confidence that his angels are on the job. A vast angelic army is on our side, watching over us.

In Acts 5, the Sadducees arrested Peter and several apostles for preaching the good news at the Jerusalem temple. But God didn't want the apostles to sit in jail. He wanted them to preach at the temple. So we read, "During the night an angel of the Lord opened the doors of the jail and brought them out" (Acts 5:19). The very next day, the apostles were right back at the temple, preaching the good news of Jesus.

In Acts 12, King Herod imprisoned Peter. Perhaps Herod had heard about Peter's previous jailbreak, because he ordered *extra* guards for

Peter—four squads of four soldiers each, a total of sixteen guards for one prisoner. But Herod could have surrounded Peter with a hundred times as many guards and it wouldn't have mattered.

In the account, Peter was bound with chains, sleeping between two soldiers, with more soldiers guarding the entrance. The angel of the Lord appeared, struck Peter on the side to wake him, and said, "Quick, get up!" Immediately, the chains fell away. The angel told Peter to get dressed and follow him out of the prison. They walked past Herod's guards, through the open gate, and out into the street. At that point, the angel left Peter—and Peter said, "Now I know without a doubt that the Lord has sent his angel and rescued me from Herod's clutches" (Acts 12:11).

God is still the Lord of hosts, and his angels still surround us today as we fight in the invisible war.

SATAN'S COMMAND STRUCTURE

Satan copied his command structure from God's command structure in heaven. This is yet another example of the principle that Satan cannot create anything new—he can only hijack what God and his servants have created. There are three aspects of Satan's command structure we should be aware of.

First: Satan's forces still retain their God-given power. When Lucifer fell from heaven, he set up his kingdom using a government system that copied what God had done in heaven. Lucifer had been the angel of light who served the throne of God. He observed the command structure of heaven, and he replicated that structure. When he and his followers fell, they were still the same powerful beings they had been in heaven—but they were no longer God's servants. They were God's enemies.

That's why Paul tells us, "Our struggle is not against flesh and blood, but against the rulers, against the authorities, against the powers of this dark world and against the spiritual forces of evil in the heavenly realms" (Ephesians 6:12). The term "heavenly realms" does not refer to the heaven where God dwells. This term refers to the atmospheric places. It is the same realm Paul speaks of when he calls Satan "the ruler of the kingdom of the air, the spirit who is now at work in those who are disobedient" (Ephesians 2:2). The King James Version uses the phrase, "the prince of the power of the air."

Remember that there are four levels of the command structure that Paul mentions in Colossians 1:16. In both the angelic hierarchy of heaven and in Satan's demonic hierarchy, there are *thrones* at the top, then *powers* (or dominions), then *rulers* (or principalities), then *authorities* (Satan's foot soldiers who wreak havoc in the world).

Satan is on the top of the pyramid, the throne level. Satan may have lost his innocence when he fell, but he did not lose his intelligence. All of the fallen angels have their own distinct personalities and characteristics. All are immortal and are not limited by time and space. There is one major difference between what Satan's forces did in heaven versus what they do now as fallen angels: They now serve and worship Lucifer instead of God.

SATAN'S AGENTS

Second: Satan has assigned an agent to your case.

I don't want that to frighten you. You never need to be frightened of Satan. Take him seriously, be aware of his strategies—but don't be afraid of Satan. Instead, make sure that Satan is afraid of you. He is a defeated foe, a toothless lion. And remember this: Satan only took one-third of the angels of heaven with him when he fell. This means that for every demon in the world, there are *two* of God's angels protecting you and watching over you.

Don't fear Satan, but *do* be aware that Satan has assigned an agent to your case. Unlike God, Satan cannot be everywhere at once.

He cannot be at your house and at my house at the same time. So Satan uses the demons under his command to carry out his plans and strategies.

I know of only two recorded instances where Satan made a personal appearance. The first was in the Garden of Eden, when Satan appeared to Adam and Eve in the guise of a serpent. The second was when Satan personally tempted Jesus in the wilderness. He could not leave that task to an underling. He had to do it himself because he wanted to stop Jesus from going to the cross. He wanted to thwart God's plan for redeeming the human race. So Satan showed up in the wilderness and performed those three temptations.

People often say, "Satan tempted me." But when we feel tempted to sin, it is almost certainly one of Satan's foot soldiers tempting us—an agent that Satan has assigned to us. Satan does not perform day-to-day operations on people today any more than the CEO of Apple stands behind the counter to personally sell you an iPhone. Satan leaves the routine temptations to his underlings.

But don't underestimate his underlings! They will harass you, frustrate you, oppress you, and entice you. That is why Paul tells us that "our struggle is not against flesh and blood," but against rulers, authorities, powers, and spiritual forces of evil.

And I hate to tell you this, but demons are diligent, hard-working, and committed to their task. They are disciplined and blindly obedient to Satan. They are not lazy. That's why we must be vigilant at all times.

How do we maintain a mindset of vigilance? We do so by inviting the Holy Spirit to come in and take residence in our lives. Every day, we must renew his presence in our lives, inviting the Holy Spirit to fill us and take control of us. When the Holy Spirit lives in us, we are spiritually alert and vigilant. He will call upon angels to protect you when the need arises. He will alert you to the danger of temptation.

We must pray daily for a vigilant sensitivity to hear the voice of the Holy Spirit within us. We must listen for the soft voice that says, "Watch out, there's danger here." Vigilance also means practicing obedience to the voice of the Holy Spirit, because disobedience results in grieving and quenching the Spirit. When we disobey him, we make it harder to hear his voice. Praying, listening to the Spirit's voice, and obeying the Spirit's leading—that's what it means to be vigilant.

UNWITTING COLLABORATORS

Third: Satan sometimes uses Christians as unwitting collaborators.

I once heard a story (whether it actually happened or not, I can't say) about a man who was on his way to a Halloween costume party. He was not a spiritually discerning man, and he thought it would be amusing to attend the party dressed as a devil. Of course, his costume was the cultural cliché of a devil—red suit, horns, tail, and pitchfork. (I'm sure that Satan enjoys the fact that people have this silly stereotype in mind when they think of him.)

On the way to the party, the man's car broke down. A short distance away was a church. The lights were on, and a meeting was taking place. The man figured that he would surely find someone to help him at the church.

So he walked to the building in his red devil costume and opened the door. People turned and looked at him—then they leaped for the doors and windows as fast as they could.

But one little old lady wasn't afraid of him. She walked up to the man in the devil suit, shook her cane at him, and said, "Listen here, devil, I've been a member in this church for many years—but I've always been on your side."

The truth is that there are people in the church who are unwitting collaborators with Satan. Their lack of discernment allows Satan to use them for his purposes. It is so tragic to see professing Christians fraternizing with the enemy. In the military, a soldier who fraternizes with the enemy is called a traitor. In the church, there are unfortunately many professing Christians who have become traitors to the cause of Christ and his kingdom.

Never assume it can't happen to you. Any believer could fall prey to an attitude of arrogance, self-righteousness, or pride—and become an unwitting collaborator with the enemy.

It happened to Peter, the chief apostle. After Jesus told his disciples that he must go to Jerusalem and die, Peter took Jesus aside and argued with him, saying, "Never, Lord! This shall never happen to you!"

And Jesus replied, "Get behind me, Satan! You are a stumbling block to me; you do not have in mind the concerns of God, but merely human concerns" (see Matthew 16:21-23).

Jesus wasn't saying that Peter was literally Satan. But when Peter tried to argue Jesus out of doing God's will, he became an unwitting collaborator with Satan. He was doing Satan's bidding, not God's. He was serving Satan's purpose, not God's. Satan was using Peter to hinder God's plan of redemption and salvation for lost humanity.

If Satan could dupe Peter into collaborating with him, he can fool anyone—including you or me. He can use any of us when we don't resist him. He can use any of us when we don't flee from temptation. That's why we need to understand Satan's strategies. Our ignorance of Satan's designs and tricks opens a doorway into our lives.

The book of Hebrews tells us that angels are "ministering spirits sent to serve those who will inherit salvation" (Hebrews 1:14). When you invite the Holy Spirit to strengthen you on a moment-by-moment basis, the Spirit will send angels to minister to you—and to send the demons fleeing. As the psalmist reminds us, "The LORD is with me; I will not be afraid. What can mere mortals do to me?" (Psalm 118:6).

OUR RELENTLESS FOE

Whether we like it or not, whether we want it or not, and whether we believe it or not, we are at war. If Jesus Christ is your Lord and Savior, you are in a state of war with Satan. The devil will attack you again and again—and you must prepare yourself for those attacks.

Although Satan is a defeated foe, he refuses to accept defeat. He refuses to lay down his weapons. He is relentless—and when he's not attacking, he's plotting the next attack.

You may think that the relentlessness and warlike nature of Satan is bad news—and it is. But the good news is that Satan and his evil forces can be defeated by God's children *if they equip themselves for battle*.

Demonic forces are like terrorists (or maybe I should say, terrorists are like demonic forces). Both terrorists and demons play dirty. There is no Geneva Convention for spiritual warfare. Both terrorists and demons look for vulnerability and weakness. They attack without warning. They do not fight fairly, and they play by no rules. They are utterly ruthless.

Though Satan leads the forces of darkness, he disguises himself as an angel of light. He wears this disguise in order to deceive us and lull us into a false sense of safety. He whispers ideas and temptations to us that sound good, and even godly, but which hide a demonic agenda.

Satan quietly suggests to us that there are no absolute moral standards, and that the temptation he has placed before us is only a "minor sin." Satan infiltrates well-intentioned causes, movements, and even churches, appealing to their good intentions while undermining their once-noble purpose. Satan inspires his human agents to use flattery to manipulate us into doing things that are harmful or sinful.

As a master of disguise, Satan has an array of false teachings and ideologies that seem "enlightened" and even "godly," but contain deadly spiritual poisons. He encourages us to rationalize "small" compromises that, over time, lead us into major apostasy and error. He is able to deceive believers into thinking that gossip is really "sharing a prayer request" or that judgmentalism is really a "zeal for righteousness."

Many people, including many Christians, have been deceived by Satan's "angel of light" disguise. By the time they realize their error, the damage is complete—and lives have been ruined.

DON'T TAKE GOD'S GRACE FOR GRANTED

Finally, I appeal to you *not* to take the grace and the mercy of God for granted. The Bible calls this the sin of presumption. Don't presume on the grace of God. Don't take it for granted. Don't give the enemy room to work in your life.

The apostle John tells us, "Dear friends, do not believe every spirit, but test the spirits to see whether they are from God, because many false prophets have gone out into the world" (1 John 4:1). Don't be gullible. Don't believe every preacher you see on TV or on YouTube. Many false prophets preach false gospels in order to elevate or enrich themselves. Fact-check what they claim by comparing their word against God's Word. Don't be fooled—or you may find that you have become an unwitting collaborator with the enemy.

Make sure that Satan cannot find an unlocked door into your life. No one in Satan's chain of command can force open a closed door. They have to wait for that door to be opened from the inside. When you shut these doors by the power of God, you know that your enemy cannot break it down because the Holy Spirit stands guard—and he sends his angels to ensure that the door remains bolted and locked.

4

ARMORED FOR BATTLE

The full armor of God is not something you can put on and then take off. It is something you put on and keep on. You never take it off. The full armor of God is not a football uniform you put on before the big game and then take off again after the game when you head to the showers. The full armor of God is a permanent fixture. It's God's continuous provision of power for our daily lives.

ARMORED FOR BATTLE

In 2001, Dr. Aaron Westrick, the research director for Second Chance Body Armor, became alarmed at what his tests revealed. Second Chance was the largest manufacturer of body armor in the United States, which meant that more federal, state, and local law enforcement officers wore Second Chance body armor than any other brand. Westrick's tests showed that the Zylon-brand fiber material, which was intended to stop bullets and save officers' lives, tended to deteriorate rapidly when exposed to hot and humid weather.

Westrick reported his findings to the corporate leaders at Second Chance Body Armor and urged them to inform law enforcement agencies of the problem and withdraw the product from the market. Corporate officials ignored his recommendations.

As one report concluded, after Westrick told Second Chance and the manufacturer of Zylon of his findings, "the companies agreed between themselves to hide the results of Westrick's tests and even denied Westrick access to his own research." Westrick soon found he was excluded from company meetings. He suspected that a deliberate cover-up was underway.

In 2003, a police officer was shot and killed in California. In a separate incident, a police officer was permanently injured in a shooting.

Both wore body armor containing Zylon fiber. In 2004, Westrick filed a lawsuit against his employer under the False Claims Act of 1863, a federal law that holds companies liable for defrauding the government. Second Chance fired him soon after he filed the lawsuit.

The Department of Justice warned law enforcement agencies that the Second Chance body armor did not meet federal standards and should be replaced. The legal fight to hold Second Chance and other defendants accountable lasted eighteen years and was finally settled in 2022.[1]

How would you feel if you put your life on the line every day, trusting your body armor to keep you alive—only to find out that the material that protects you from bullets begins to deteriorate when the weather gets warm and humid? How would you feel if you or someone close to you was killed or wounded because of defective body armor—and the manufacturers knew it was defective but covered up the truth?

The armor that our mighty Lord has provided for our protection will never fail. It doesn't deteriorate in hot weather—or in the heat of spiritual warfare. The armor God gives us is all the equipment we will ever need to live the Christian life and fight the Christian fight.

THE FULL ARMOR OF GOD

In Ephesians 6, the apostle Paul gives us a complete owner's manual of the protective gear we need to achieve victory in the invisible war. He writes:

> Be strong in the Lord and in his mighty power. Put on the full armor of God, so that you can take your stand against the devil's schemes. For our struggle is not against flesh and blood, but against the rulers, against the authorities, against the powers of this dark world and against the

spiritual forces of evil in the heavenly realms. Therefore put on the full armor of God, so that when the day of evil comes, you may be able to stand your ground, and after you have done everything, to stand. Stand firm then, with the belt of truth buckled around your waist, with the breastplate of righteousness in place, and with your feet fitted with the readiness that comes from the gospel of peace. In addition to all this, take up the shield of faith, with which you can extinguish all the flaming arrows of the evil one. Take the helmet of salvation and the sword of the Spirit, which is the word of God (Ephesians 6:10-17).

He begins with the words, "Be strong…" Be strong in your own strength? In your self-reliance? In your hard work? No! "Be strong in the Lord and in his mighty power" (Ephesians 6:10).

Why? Because spiritual warfare is the one thing in life that you dare not attempt on your own. Our battle is not against flesh and blood, but against the rulers, authorities, and spiritual forces of evil in the invisible, unseen realms. If we were to battle human beings, we might be able to match them in physical strength or intellectual prowess or strategic thinking. But the invisible war is not a fight between equals. You and I are no match for the cunning supernatural forces of Satan and his demons.

The heart of Paul's letter to the Ephesians is this profound truth: As believers we are *in Christ*. We are one with him. His life is our life. His power is our power. His truth is our truth. His way is our way. And, above all, *his strength is our strength*.

Our own strength is totally inadequate. That's why Paul tells us to be *strong in the Lord*. It doesn't matter how strong you and I are. All that matters is: What is the source of our strength? If that source is Jesus, then we will have victory. In fact, the victory is completely assured because Jesus already won the victory when he cried out, "It is finished!" from the cross.

How can we secure Jesus's victory and strength for our lives? Paul tells us in the next verse: "Put on the full armor of God, so that you can take your stand against the devil's schemes" (Ephesians 6:11).

The full armor of God is not something you can put on and then take off. It is something you put on and keep on. You never take it off. The full armor of God is not a football uniform you put on before the big game and then take off again after the game when you head to the showers. The full armor of God is a permanent fixture. It's God's continuous provision of power for our daily lives.

Some writers have suggested that Paul may have been observing the Roman jailer who was guarding him in prison. Paul may have looked at the different pieces and parts of the Roman armor as he was pondering his spiritual analogy. Through this analogy, Paul was telling us that God, in his mercy, has given us all the spiritual equipment we need to win the invisible war. We have *everything* we need *if* we will avail ourselves of it.

Why did God give us this armor? Paul says, "So that you can take your stand against the devil's schemes." When you see evil, corruption, deception, and gaslighting in politics, you are seeing the devil's schemes at work. When you see school officials or teachers slipping evil ideologies into the school curriculum or placing pornography on the school library shelves, you are seeing the devil's schemes at work. When you see churches that preach that the Bible is made up of myths, that Jesus was merely a good human teacher, and that the resurrection is just a metaphor, you are seeing the devil's schemes at work.

In the first five chapters of Ephesians, Paul calls us to walk worthy of our Christian calling, to walk in humility rather than pride, in unity rather than divisiveness, in love rather than lust, in the Spirit rather than drunkenness, in mutual submission rather than selfishness. But we cannot walk this way and live this way in our own power.

If Paul had ended the letter to the Ephesians at chapter 5, we would have no idea how to carry out his instructions in those first five chapters. Thank God, he went on to write Ephesians 6, which gives us the key to living out the instructions in Ephesians 1 through 5. And that key is the full armor of God.

THE BELT OF TRUTH

If you have been a Christian for a number of years, you have probably read Ephesians 6 many times before. You have probably heard again and again about the full armor of God. The problem we face with a familiar passage of Scripture is that we assume we know all there is to know about it—and there is the risk we will tune out and miss deeper layers of meaning. We often fail to realize that a single passage of Scripture usually has many levels of meaning. Whenever we return to a familiar passage, we are likely to discover new truths that we never understood before *if* we are attentive and ask the Holy Spirit to reveal new truths to us from his Word.

In Ephesians 6, Paul lists seven pieces of armor that God has provided for our protection in the invisible war. Each piece provides a unique form of protection against the onslaught of Satan and his demons. This armor is our identity and our survival kit.

The public ministry of the Lord Jesus Christ was characterized by his use of the full armor of God. He wore this armor when he answered Satan in the wilderness. He wore this armor when he answered his critics and opponents, the scribes and Pharisees.

If Jesus wore this armor in his spiritual battles, how much more do we need to cover ourselves from head to foot—from helmet to shield to shoes to sword—in the full armor of God?

The first piece of armor is *the belt of truth*. Paul writes, "Stand firm then, with the belt of truth buckled around your waist" (Ephesians 6:14).

Roman soldiers wore tunics—square pieces of cloth with openings for the head and arms. The tunic would flow loosely around the soldier's body when the soldier was standing at ease. But when it was time for battle, a soldier could not let the tunic get in his way. Combat in the Roman era was frequently a hand-to-hand, sword-to-sword battle. So Roman soldiers would wrap a thick leather belt around themselves. They would cinch it and buckle it tightly, so that the tunic would be held against their bodies.

Having your clothes tucked inside a protective belt is a sign of readiness. A serious-minded soldier must always be ready to leap into battle at a moment's notice. He must have his clothing tucked inside his belt to keep his tunic from hampering his movements.

The belt of truth keeps Christian soldiers from stumbling. Without the belt of truth, you might fall for false teaching. The belt of truth enables you to discern truth from falsehood. The belt of truth enables you to smell false doctrine a mile away—and makes it possible for you to run away from false teachers and their lies. For Christians, being ready for battle starts with the truth. Being buckled up by the belt of truth is the make-or-break key to spiritual victory.

There are many people today who used to believe and teach the Bible as God's Word, but now they have fallen away from the faith. What happened to them? They ceased to take seriously the vital importance of the belt of truth.

Many Christians are very involved in Christian fellowship, in church attendance, in volunteering for church outreach programs and ministries to the poor, yet they have not buckled on the belt of truth. They are not absolutely committed to accurate biblical teaching. They are tossed about by every wind of doctrine. They are easily deceived by deceptive spirits and false teachers.

The belt of truth must be a permanent fixture of the full armor of God. We must never remove it. Think of the belt of truth this way: The tunic the Roman soldiers wore is comparable to the cares, concerns, and affairs of this world. Just as the Roman soldiers didn't want their sword-fighting arm to be encumbered by a tunic flapping in the breeze, we don't want to be hindered by worldly cares. We need to wrap the truth of God's Word tightly around us so that we are not distracted in our spiritual battles.

These days, you'll hear many people—including some preachers and teachers—demeaning the Word of God. They will tell you that God's Word is unreliable, or that it's not meant to be taken literally, or that parts of it can be chucked out and ignored because it's no longer relevant to our times. But God's Word is the truth. It stands forever regardless of what some apostate preacher says.

For decades I've been saying that it's harder to live for Christ than to die for Christ. The longer I live, the more convinced I am of the truth of that statement. To live in faithful obedience to the Word of God while believers all around us are falling away from the faith—that's hard, that's painful, that's lonely. But that's what it means to buckle on the belt of truth.

Anyone who fails to buckle it on, or anyone who unbuckles it and takes it off, has left himself or herself vulnerable to Satan's schemes.

THE BREASTPLATE OF RIGHTEOUSNESS

After the belt of truth, Paul tells us to put on the second piece of armor, *the breastplate of righteousness*. We must go into battle, he writes, "with the breastplate of righteousness in place" (Ephesians 6:14).

The modern equivalent of the old Roman-era breastplate would be the body armor or bulletproof vest that law enforcement officers wear today. Roman soldiers would never think of stepping onto the battlefield without that breastplate. It protected the vital organs—heart, lungs, and intestines—from enemy swords. The breastplate often consisted of a sheet of hard leather covered with a metal layer. It was skillfully hammered out to conform to the contours of the soldier's body.

In Old Testament times, the *heart* represented the mind, the seat of the will. For example, Genesis 6:5 speaks of "the thoughts of the human *heart*," and Psalm 14:1 says, "The fool says in his *heart*, 'There is no God.'" So the heart was viewed as the location of the mind.

And what represented the seat of human emotions? The *bowels* or intestines. Genesis 43:30 tells us that Joseph, after he became the prime minister of Egypt, was "deeply moved" when he saw his brother Benjamin for the first time in years. But in the original Hebrew, this verse literally tells us that Joseph's "bowels yearned" for his brother. Similarly, in 1 Kings 3:26, the story of Solomon judging between the two women who claimed the same baby as their own, the Hebrew text tells us that the real mother's "bowels yearned" for her baby.

These phrases sound strange to us today, so modern translations leave out the word *bowels* and give us the essential meaning. But it's helpful to remember that the bowels were viewed as the location of the emotions. It's helpful because the Roman breastplate protected these two vital parts of the body, the heart and the bowels.

Paul is telling us that the breastplate of righteousness protects the *heart* and *bowels* of the soul, which are the mind and the emotions. And where does Satan aim his most vicious attacks? At our minds and our emotions. Satan continually seeks to cloud our minds with false doctrines, false information, and sinful thoughts. He also tries to confuse us with inappropriate emotions, from selfish resentment and anger to a false sense of guilt and shame.

One way Satan tries to confuse both our minds and emotions is with slogans. Satan loves slogans because they are short, easy to remember, and they can easily short-circuit logical thought. Slogans often *seem* to make sense when you first hear them, but if you stop to think them over, you realize they are really nonsense.

For many years, gay rights activists have carried signs or shouted chants of "Born this way!" or "We're here, we're queer, get used to it!" (or, more ominously, "We're here, we're queer, and we're coming for your children!"). The transgender community—people who are tragically confused about whether they are a man in a woman's body or a woman in a man's body—have adopted the slogan "Trans rights are human rights."

But I think one of the most dangerous slogans Satan has inspired is "Love is love." The false idea behind this seemingly redundant slogan is that all forms of love are equally valid and worthy of respect, regardless of the sexual orientation involved. It's a phrase intended to end the discussion and prevent people from thinking more carefully about the subject. It's all-inclusive because it applies equally to the lesbians, gays, bisexuals, transexuals, and queers who make up the LGBTQ+ community.

But there's a problem that many in that community didn't think of when they started chanting "Love is love." In recent years, pedophiles—monstrous people who sexually exploit children—have also started chanting "Love is love." Why? Because they see that slogan as a way to change minds and defend their soul-destroying abuse of innocent children.

Because Satan is committed to confusing our thinking and distorting our emotions and affections, he has inspired the entire secular-left community—in academia, the media, Hollywood, and the leftist political establishment—to chant this insipid-yet-toxic slogan. It sounds so reasonable: Love is love. Who could be against love? If you oppose this slogan, then you must be in favor of hate! The satanic scheming behind this slogan is blatantly obvious.

I have even heard people say, "The Jesus I know does *not* care about my sex life. After all, the Bible says, 'God is love.'" Satan is an expert at perverting the meaning of God's Word, as we saw when he tempted Jesus in the wilderness. He specializes in erasing God's meaning from our minds and replacing it with the perverted thinking of this world. He wants us to joke about our sins instead of mourning them. He wants us to rationalize sin instead of confessing it and repenting of it.

God has given us the breastplate of righteousness to protect our minds and our emotions from the corrupting influence of this world and the attacks of Satan. But what is the breastplate of righteousness, and how do we put it on?

The breastplate of righteousness is not self-righteousness. In fact, our self-righteousness is nothing but filthy rags.

And the breastplate of righteousness is not the righteousness of God that is imputed to us when we receive Jesus as our Lord and Savior. The imputed righteousness of God is already ours at the moment of conversion. As believers, we are clothed in the righteousness of God at all times. God's imputed righteousness protects us from hell. We can't put on what we are already wearing.

So what is this piece of armor Paul calls the breastplate of righteousness? It's daily obedience to the Word of God. In fact, our continual obedience to God is the visible evidence that we have received the imputed righteousness of God. It's God's imputed righteousness that enables us to practice obedience and put on the breastplate of righteousness.

How do we live obediently every day? We are assailed by temptations within and without, hour by hour, minute by minute. The moment you say, "I've decided to live in obedience from now on"—you find yourself tripped up by some temptation or sin.

You can't live in obedience in your own strength. Human willpower is as weak as water. Face it. You are powerless to put on the breastplate of righteousness in your own strength. But the Holy Spirit, who first convicted you of sin and your need for a Savior, can put the breastplate of righteousness on you every day.

Putting on the breastplate of righteousness means that you lean completely on God's strength for your obedience. By prayer, you offer God your total dependence on him. The moment you are tempted, you call out to God and ask him for the strength to flee temptation. When temptation returns, you pray again. And again. And again, as many times as it takes.

Eventually, Satan's agents will leave you alone—at least for a while. They will realize that they can't break you down because you are protected by the breastplate of righteousness.

YOUR GOSPEL FOOTWEAR

Next, Paul urges you to stand firm "with your feet fitted with the readiness that comes from the gospel of peace" (Ephesians 6:15).

Today, we have shoes for every occasion and activity—athletic shoes of every kind, hiking boots, leisure shoes, dress shoes, and on and on. Soldiers need a very different kind of shoe than civilians. A soldier's mortal life may depend on having the right shoes—shoes that are tough and durable, that have a good fit and good traction, and that will be dependable during the heat of battle.

The spiritual footwear the apostle speaks of is critically important to our survival in the invisible war. Paul says our feet must be shod with "the readiness that comes from the gospel of peace." Paul has in mind an Old Testament verse:

> How beautiful on the mountains
>   are the feet of those who bring good news,
> who proclaim peace,

> who bring good tidings,
> who proclaim salvation,
> who say to Zion,
> "Your God reigns!" (Isaiah 52:7).

When Paul talks about having our feet shod with gospel readiness, he's not talking about being ready to travel. He's talking about standing firmly and immovably in one place, ready to fight our spiritual battles. He's not talking about evangelizing or taking the gospel overseas. He's talking about fighting our spiritual enemy right where we are amid pressure, opposition, and temptation.

What is "the gospel of peace"? Before we committed our lives to Jesus, we were God's enemies. We were at war with ourselves, with the people around us, and with God. But once Jesus saved us, the war was over. We became reconciled to God. At last, we had peace *with* God—and we had the peace *of* God. The gospel of peace is the truth of Jesus Christ—the good news that we have been purchased by the blood of Christ. We have been saved from sin, death, and hell. If God is for us, who can be against us?

Today, as believers, we stand confidently in God's love. We stand confidently in God's promise to fight for us. Any believer who stands in the power of Jesus has every right to be fearless. We need not live in fear of Satan. Whenever he attacks us, we can stand firm, knowing that our spiritual combat boots—our gospel readiness—make us immovable and invincible.

THE SHIELD OF FAITH

Next, Paul urges us to take up *the shield of faith*. He explains why this piece of armor is important: "In addition to all this, take up the shield of faith, with which you can extinguish all the flaming arrows of the evil one" (Ephesians 6:16). The shield must always be kept ready because the enemy is armed with flaming arrows. We must always be on a war footing, ready and prepared to fight at a moment's notice.

In Roman times, there were two common types of shields. One was a round shield about two feet in diameter, secured to the arm by two leather straps. It was a relatively lightweight shield used to fend off the sword blows of an enemy in close combat.

The other Roman shield was a larger, rectangular shied called a *scutum* in Latin, but which was invented centuries earlier by the Greeks, who called it a *thyreos*. It was made of wood covered with leather or metal, and it was carried by a central handgrip. It was about three feet wide by five feet high and designed to protect a soldier's entire body.

When Paul says, "take up the shield of faith," the Greek word he chooses for shield is *thyreos*. He's not saying we should take up the small round shield so that we can go toe to toe with Satan and battle it out with swords. He's telling us to take the large *thyreos* and shield ourselves from head to toe against the fire-tipped arrows Satan will rain down on us.

Ancient battles were incredibly brutal. Archers would wrap pitch-soaked cloth around the head of their arrow, set the pitch aflame, and then launch the flaming arrows at the enemy. Anyone who was pierced by a flaming arrow would almost certainly be incapacitated and writhing in pain, if not killed outright.

To prevent this from happening, Roman shield carriers would stand on the front line of the battlefield. They were trained to stand side by side, shield by shield, with no space between them. They could form a protective wall of shields that the enemy could not penetrate, even with a fiery hailstorm of flame-tipped arrows. The Romans would unleash a volley of arrows, then hunker down behind their shields, safe from the fury of the enemy.

We can be thankful that when Satan launches his flaming arrows against us, those arrows bounce harmlessly off our shield of faith.

What is that shield of faith we are to take up? It is absolute trust and confidence in Jesus, our Commander. This faith is not a once-and-for-all action, as when you received Jesus as your Lord and Savior. It's a faith that you must renew and exercise day after day.

It's the absolute confidence that if you open your mouth to witness to others about Jesus Christ, he will give you boldness and the words to speak. It's the absolute confidence that if God calls you to dare great things for him, he will see them through to completion. It's the absolute confidence that, even if you don't know where your next paycheck or your next meal is coming from, God will provide.

You must take up the shield of faith daily and take refuge behind it, confident that it will not fail you when Satan's fiery darts start to fall around you. Your trust in Christ began the day you accepted the free gift of salvation—and it will grow and strengthen every day as you trust him and rely on him.

Jesus never fails. He is your shield when you trust him completely. Your world may fall apart, but you can always trust him. The doctor may have given you bad news, but you can trust in the comforting care of the Great Physician. Your business may be struggling, but Jesus will always meet your needs.

THE HELMET OF SALVATION

Next, Paul urges us to put on *the helmet of salvation*. Any soldier would be out of his mind to step on to the battlefield without a helmet. Some Roman helmets were made of thick leather covered with metal. Others were made entirely of metal, and they typically consisted of a bowl to cover the skull, a neck guard in back, cheek plates along the side, and a deflector band for extra protection of the forehead. The single function of the helmet was to protect the head from injuries. That is why Paul tells us, "Take the helmet of salvation" (Ephesians 6:17).

God's Word calls this piece of armor "the helmet of salvation" because Satan aims his sword at our heads—at our security and assurance that we are truly saved. Satan wants to discourage us and cause us to doubt. He loves to dishearten believers and make them question the reality of their faith to the point of sinning and falling into unbelief.

When Paul tells us to put on the helmet of salvation, he is speaking to those who are already saved. He is not urging us to receive Christ and be saved. He assumes we are already saved, and he is urging us to remind ourselves of God's promises so that we will be encouraged and protected in battle. The armor of God is for those who are saved and are engaged in the invisible war—that is, in spiritual warfare.

Theologians have debated for years the question of the believer's security. You may have heard people refer to "eternal security" or "once saved, always saved." I was raised to believe that it's up to me to "stay saved," and that even though I was saved one day, I might lose my salvation the next day. This belief caused me many experiences of spiritual terror—of feeling that I might lose my salvation at any moment.

I cannot begin to describe my overwhelming sense of relief when I discovered the biblical truth that God's gracious gift of salvation is permanent, dependable, and irrevocable. God does *not* write my name with a pencil in the Book of Life and then erase it every time I sin. And he doesn't write my name in again when I repent—write, erase, write, erase. No, that's not how it works.

Times of discouragement and doubt can lead us to question the love and mercy of God—but thank God, his saving grace does not depend on our moods or emotional state. His saving power is dependable and secure because it's anchored in God's faithfulness, not ours.

The combination of discouragement and doubt is a psychological phenomenon that I call the "Elijah Syndrome." I think almost every believer has experienced the Elijah Syndrome, and it's important to understand how it affects us so that we don't get trapped in it. I would define the Elijah Syndrome as the discouragement that often follows a great victory, the valley we descend into after a mountaintop experience.

Elijah's victory on Mount Carmel (1 Kings 18) is one of the most dramatic stories in the Bible. Israel was divided. Some of the people worshipped Yahweh while others worshipped the Canaanite god Baal. So faithful Elijah challenged 450 prophets of Baal to a showdown on Mount Carmel. He proposed that each side prepare a sacrifice—but without lighting a fire. The deity who sent fire from heaven would be proven to be the one true God.

The pagan prophets called on Baal and performed their rituals, but there was no fire. Elijah confidently drenched his sacrifice with water—then he prayed. Immediately, God sent such a hot fire that it consumed the sacrifice, the wood, and even the stones of the altar. Elijah then commanded that the false prophets of Baal be seized and executed.

The wicked Queen Jezebel, enraged by the execution of the false prophets, sought to kill Elijah. He fled into the wilderness, exhausted and afraid. He suffered such deep depression and discouragement that he prayed for God to end his life. (I don't think Elijah really wanted to die; if he did, he could have simply returned to Jezebel, and she would have obliged him.)

God sustained Elijah through his time of despair, giving him food and rest through the aid of an angel. God revealed himself to Elijah, not in a dramatic display of power, but in a gentle whisper. That soft voice reminded Elijah that God was with him. With that reassurance, Elijah returned to his mission with renewed confidence and faith (1 Kings 19).

We all need the Lord's strength and a heavenly perspective after a great victory. Triumphs are often followed by a sense of letdown. We must remember that, from Satan's point of view, the battle is never over. We may feel at times that we have won a great battle, but Satan does not accept defeat. He merely regroups to prepare his next attack. That is why we must never let our guard down—and why we must put on the helmet of our salvation.

Satan not only seeks to discourage us in our own trials, but he also tries to bring us down when we see our Christian friends going through hard times. Years ago, I was ministering to a friend who was going through a difficult trial. As I was talking to him and praying with him, I realized I was becoming more discouraged for him than he was.

We need the helmet of salvation to guard us from discouragement. We put on the helmet of salvation by trusting the Lord's promises. Jesus said, "I give them eternal life, and they shall never perish; no one will snatch them out of my hand. My Father, who has given them to me, is greater than all; no one can snatch them out of my Father's hand" (John 10:28-29). Ephesians 4:30 tells us that the Holy Spirit has "sealed [us] for the day of redemption." And Romans 8:38-39 tells us that nothing "will be able to separate us from the love of God that is in Christ Jesus our Lord."

God has promised that our salvation has taken place once and for all. He will continue to sustain us and save us until the day we are finally home in heaven.

Now, there are some people who say, "I accepted Jesus as my Savior, so I have my 'fire escape.' Having Jesus as my Savior is good enough—I don't want to obey him as Lord. I'm going to live for myself. I'm going to sin to my heart's content, and then when I die… well, I won't have a great reward, but at least I'll go to heaven."

Such a person should seriously search within and ask, "Did I really make a serious commitment of my life to Jesus? Was I ever truly saved to begin with? How can Jesus be my Savior if I do not let him be the Lord of my life?" That's why Peter writes:

> Make every effort to add to your faith goodness; and to goodness, knowledge; and to knowledge, self-control; and to self-control, perseverance; and to perseverance, godliness; and to godliness, mutual affection; and to mutual affection, love. For if you possess these qualities in increasing measure, they will keep you from being ineffective and unproductive in your knowledge of our Lord Jesus Christ. But whoever does not have them is nearsighted and blind, forgetting that they have been cleansed from their past sins. Therefore, my brothers and sisters, make every effort to confirm your calling and election. For if you do these things, you will never stumble, and you will receive a rich welcome into the eternal kingdom of our Lord and Savior Jesus Christ (2 Peter 1:5-11).

The moment we place our trust in Jesus, he saves us from the penalty of sin. As we trust in Jesus day by day, his promises assure us that we are no longer slaves to sin. His promises also assure us of eternity in heaven with Jesus, which is the ultimate object of salvation.

The Bible speaks of salvation in three ways: We were *saved in the past*, when we came to Christ the first time in repentance and faith. We are daily being *saved in the present* by trusting the promises of God. And we will be *saved in the future* when we are safely home in heaven with the Lord.

THE SWORD OF THE SPIRIT

Paul gives us the final piece of protective equipment for the invisible war, *the sword of the Spirit*. A sword is not a piece of defensive armor but a weapon that has both defensive and offensive uses: "and the sword of the Spirit, which is the word of God" (Ephesians 6:17).

Swords come in different sizes and shapes. The Greek word Paul uses in this verse is *machaira*, which refers to a relatively small sword, about eight inches in length. This was a very common sword in the Roman army. It was the primary weapon the Romans used for hand-to-hand combat. They carried the sword in a sheath attached to their belts.

The phrase "sword of the Spirit" might also be translated "spiritual sword," suggesting that it is a spiritual weapon to be used against a spiritual enemy. Paul is telling us that the sword of the Spirit originates with God. It is not a human invention. It is our roadmap for every path in life. It is a chart for every sea. It is medicine for every sickness. It is the balm for every wound.

The sword of the Spirit is the Word of God, whose author is the Holy Spirit. It is infallible and contains no error. It is complete. It is authoritative. I do not judge the Word of God. It judges me.

The sword of the Spirit is powerful and effective. It never returns empty. It offers us limitless resources and blessings. It is the fountain of God's wisdom for our lives. It is a source of our joy, strength, and spiritual growth.

The Old Testament tells us, "Your word is a lamp for my feet, a light on my path" (Psalm 119:105). And the New Testament tells us, "The word of God is alive and active. Sharper than any double-edged sword, it penetrates even to dividing soul and spirit, joints and marrow; it judges the thoughts and attitudes of the heart" (Hebrews 4:12).

The Word of God, the sword of the Spirit, guides our steps when we lose our way so we can return to Jesus to be restored to service. Like a literal sword of steel, the sword of the Spirit is a defensive weapon as well as an offensive weapon. It is capable of both dealing blows against our enemy and fending off Satan's onslaught.

How do we use the sword of the Spirit offensively? How do we use the Word of God to strike a blow against Satan? Not by attacking Satan directly. No, God's Word becomes a powerful offensive weapon against Satan when we proclaim it to the lost, when we use it to witness to the people around us, when we lead our neighbors and coworkers and colleagues to Jesus by the power of God's Word.

When the Word of God is faithfully proclaimed, it brings judgment against lies and transforms lives. It shatters delusions and leads people out of darkness and into the light. It turns sadness into gladness, despair into hope, stagnation into growth, immobility into momentum, and failure into success. When we teach and preach God's Word accurately and boldly, people find salvation. The sword of the Spirit cuts a swath of heavenly light through Satan's kingdom of darkness.

The sword of the Spirit is our supreme weapon in the invisible war. During the temptation in the wilderness, Jesus wielded the sword of the Spirit to deflect Satan's attack. When Satan twisted the Scriptures, Jesus corrected him and countered his lies with biblical truth.

When Satan tempted Jesus by telling him to turn stones into bread, Jesus quoted Deuteronomy 8:3, saying, "It is written: 'Man shall not live on bread alone, but on every word that comes from the mouth of God'" (Matthew 4:4).

When Satan twisted the meaning of a passage from the Psalms, telling Jesus to throw himself from the heights of the Temple so that the angels would save him, Jesus quoted Deuteronomy 6:16, saying, "It is also written: 'Do not put the Lord your God to the test'" (Matthew 4:7).

And when Satan offered Jesus all the kingdoms of the world if he would worship Satan (and it was a legitimate offer, because Satan controls all the systems of this world), Jesus quoted Deuteronomy 6:13, saying, "Away from me, Satan! For it is written: 'Worship the Lord your God, and serve him only'" (Matthew 4:10).

If Jesus relied on the sword of the Spirit in his duel with Satan, how much more should we? No believer has an excuse for not reading and heeding and obeying the Word of God. We cannot plead ignorance. We can only confess our neglect. And neglect makes us vulnerable to delusions and lies.

So listen to Paul's warning. Heed it and implement it in your daily walk with God. Be strong in the Lord and in his mighty power—and put on the full armor of God, so that you can take your stand against Satan's schemes.

5

VIGILANCE IN WARTIME

We don't like to think of Satan prowling and tracking us, looking for an opportunity to pounce. But that is reality. That is why God does not call us to be comfortable—he calls us to be vigilant. He warns us, "Be alert and of sober mind."

VIGILANCE IN WARTIME

I am not an expert in animal behavior, but I am told that lions are generally quiet animals. They only roar under three conditions.

First, lions are very territorial, so they roar when they sense another lion is intruding on their territory. They roar to warn intruders away.

Second, lions are nervous, high-strung, and sensitive to noise. So lions roar at the flash of lightning and the crash of thunder. The atmospheric violence of lightning and thunder is one of the few things that can make a lion feel fear—and cause him to roar.

Third, a lion will roar after he has taken down his prey. In fact, this is when a lion roars the loudest. He was tense and silent the whole time he was tracking his prey. He didn't want to frighten his prey. But once his prey is trapped and under his control, the lion is filled with the thrill of triumph—and he unleashes a roar of victory.

The apostle Peter warns us, "Be alert and of sober mind. Your enemy the devil prowls around like a roaring lion looking for someone to devour" (1 Peter 5:8). Remember, a lion doesn't roar while he's tracking his prey. Even though Peter compares Satan to a "roaring lion," he first describes Satan as prowling around. While Satan prowls around, he is stealthy and careful not to frighten his prey into fleeing. He doesn't want us to be aware of him until it is too late. Only after he pounces on us and pins us to the ground does Satan roar over us in victory.

CALLED TO BE VIGILANT

We don't like to think of Satan prowling and tracking us, looking for an opportunity to pounce. But that is reality. That is why God does not call us to be comfortable—he calls us to be vigilant. He warns us, "Be alert and of sober mind."

I have learned to expect Satan's attacks at all times. In fact, I become very concerned if I go for any length of time without an attack from the enemy of my soul. I really do, because when things are too quiet, when it's been too long since I have suffered an attack by Satan, I know he's planning something big.

What do I do when Satan seems quiet and hidden, when I see no sign of his attack? I assume he is prowling and quietly stalking me—and I *intensify* my prayer time. I want to make sure I'm not lulled to sleep by a false sense of security. I've learned over the years not to take the peaceful, quiet times of my life for granted.

When I was a young Christian, I was ignorant of Satan's ways. I didn't realize Satan was stalking me, and that I was engaged in an invisible war. When everything in my life seemed peaceful and serene, I assumed I was not engaged in a struggle. I naively believed this was the normal state of the Christian life.

But no, the Christian life is a struggle, a state of war. You don't have the choice whether to be in the invisible war or not. Your enemy is stalking you. He's at war with you whether you like it or not. If you don't want to be a victim, you need to be vigilant at all times—including the times of tranquility in your life.

WHEN DID THE WAR BEGIN?

There is no neutrality in the invisible war. There is no "Switzerland" in spiritual warfare. You are either in the kingdom of God or the kingdom of Satan.

You and I became the enemies of Satan the moment we said yes to Jesus. When you committed your life to Christ, Satan lost you as his follower—and as his future companion in the lake of fire. Your allegiance to Jesus is an insult to Satan. When you received eternal life as a free gift of God's grace, you kicked Satan in the teeth—and he will never forgive you for it.

When you are saved, Satan doesn't shrug it off and say, "Oh well, you win some and you lose some. You can't win them all." No, Satan becomes enraged—and he sends one of his agents after you. Why? Because he wants to make you ineffective for Jesus. He wants to prevent you from living the life of faith. He wants to keep you from growing in the faith and becoming more and more like Christ.

Satan can never separate you from God and his love. But Satan wants to keep you ignorant of the *power* of God. He wants to prevent you from praying and seeking the filling of the Holy Spirit. He wants to keep you from relying on the mercy and grace of God. He wants to keep you mired in defeat and shame, paralyzed by sins that Jesus died for and has already forgiven.

There is a powerful verse tucked away in one of the epistles of John that you should memorize, bookmark in your Bible, and post on your refrigerator and the dashboard of your car. John warns his readers about false teachers who are in the world and even in the church—people who preach the message of the Antichrist. But John does not want his readers to be afraid of false teachers. Here's why: "You, dear children, are from God and have overcome them, because the one who is in you is greater than the one who is in the world" (1 John 4:4).

Who is "the one who is in the world"? Satan. And who is "the one who is in you"? Jesus the Lord!

If all you know is Satan and his plans and strategies, you will be terrified. But if you focus on knowing Jesus and his infinite power and his amazing plans for your life, you will be fearless. You will live each day with peace, victory, and joy. You will know that Jesus, who lives in you, is infinitely more powerful than the foul spirit who rules this age.

NEVER NEGOTIATE WITH SATAN

I suspect that, even as you are reading these words, one of Satan's agents may be whispering in your ear, "You certainly don't believe all this nonsense about the devil, do you? This is the twenty-first century! This is the age of the internet and space travel and robotic cars! All that superstitious talk about the devil and his demons is straight out of the Dark Ages. It's okay to think of Satan as a metaphor or a symbol—but no one takes that stuff literally anymore."

If you have had such thoughts as you have been reading this book, it may well be that Satan's agents are on the case, trying to talk you out of believing what God's Word says about the invisible war that rages around us. I would encourage you to be very careful when you hear the voice of the enemy. I suggest you don't engage in debates or negotiations with that voice.

Satan and his demons are much like a talking grizzly bear in a story I once heard.

A hunter came upon a grizzly bear in the woods—and he raised his gun to shoot the bear. But the grizzly bear astonished the hunter by opening his mouth to speak. "Please, don't shoot," the bear said. "Violence never solved anything. Let's sit down and negotiate. Tell me what you want, I'll tell you what I want, and maybe we can agree on a compromise."

The hunter lowered his gun and said, "Well, I could really use a fur coat for the winter."

"A fur coat?" the bear said. "No problem. All I want is a full stomach." So, in the process of their negotiation, the hunter got his fur coat—in a manner of speaking. And the grizzly bear walked away with a full stomach.

Friend in Christ, you can no more negotiate with Satan than you can negotiate with a grizzly bear. Satan doesn't want to compromise with you. He wants to be worshipped in place of God. That's why he rebelled and fell from heaven. Even though he was defeated on the cross, he has never given up his ambition to receive worship from you and the entire human race.

BE SOBER MINDED

Satan was defanged and declawed by Jesus at the cross. He can never challenge God again—but he can defeat God's people if they unwisely listen to him or negotiate with him. That is why Peter warns us, "Your enemy the devil prowls around like a roaring lion looking for someone to devour." Peter knew from firsthand experience how it feels to fall into Satan's trap.

In Luke 22, a scene takes place shortly before the crucifixion. Jesus tells Simon Peter, "Simon, Simon, Satan has asked to sift all of you as wheat. But I have prayed for you, Simon, that your faith may not fail. And when you have turned back, strengthen your brothers."

Peter, in his prideful self-confidence, replies, "Lord, I am ready to go with you to prison and to death." Peter's self-confidence was the unlocked back door Satan used to gain entrance into Peter's will.

Jesus said, "I tell you, Peter, before the rooster crows today, you will deny three times that you know me" (see Luke 22:31-34).

And it happened just as Jesus predicted. During our Lord's trial,

Peter denied knowing Jesus—and even bound his final denial with an oath.

As all this was going on, somewhere in the invisible realm where spiritual warfare takes place, Satan roared with triumph: "I have your man, Jesus! I have your chief disciple right where I want him!"

The Bible tells us that, after his third denial, Peter went out and wept bitterly. Satan's sifting of Peter, which Jesus had predicted, had just begun. After the sifting of fear and denial came the sifting of shame and self-condemnation. Peter was sure he had proven himself unworthy of his Lord. He may have even considered suicide—but thank God, he did not surrender to self-destructive impulses as Judas did. Peter survived being sifted by Satan—and he went on to become the leader of the early church.

That is why Peter could speak from the crucible of his own painful experience, saying in effect, "Look out! Be sober minded! Take Satan seriously. He is prowling around—and you could be his next victim!"

What does it mean to be sober minded? Most people associate being "sober" with not being drunk. Understand, you don't have to do anything to be sober. You don't have to go to school and take courses on being sober. You don't have to go to the gym and pump iron to be sober. You don't have to do anything but *not drink*.

A sober person has normal judgment, good physical balance, and quick reaction time. A drunk person has impaired judgment, is unsteady on his feet, and is slow to react in an emergency. Because his judgment is impaired, a drunk person is frequently self-deceived. He says, "I feel fine to drive. Where are my keys?" And that's why so many people are killed by drunk drivers every year.

Being spiritually sober is similar to being physically sober. It doesn't take any physical or mental effort to be spiritually sober. All you have to do is rest in the power of the Holy Spirit. All you have to do is not live in disobedience to God.

Disobedience to the Word of God is spiritual drunkenness. When you live in disobedience, you experience impaired moral judgment, your life becomes unbalanced and unsteady, and you are slow to react in times of crisis. When we are not spiritually sober, we are unable to see life from God's perspective. We are unable to recognize and avoid Satan's traps. We become flippant and careless about spiritual and moral issues in our lives.

Satan can't defeat God, so he will try to get to you and me. He will try to get us drunk on sin and disobedience. He will try to impair our spiritual judgment. I have seen Satan conquer careless Christians again and again. Please don't let this happen to you. Please don't become a casualty in the invisible war.

SIN IN YOUR CAMP

I have heard some unwise pastors say that the Old Testament is no longer relevant in today's world. But the Old Testament was written for our instruction, and it is filled with powerful insights and warnings for our lives today.

The life of Joshua, the hand-picked successor to Moses, contains a number of warnings for us today. In Joshua 5 and 6, God gives Joshua instructions for conquering the city of Jericho. Joshua was supposed to have his army march around the city walls in silence with the Ark of the Covenant at the head of the procession, day after day for six days. Then, on the seventh day, they were to circle the city seven times—and on the seventh time, they would all shout. Clearly, these instructions made no military sense.

But Joshua obeyed. His army carried out God's instructions—and when the people shouted, the walls of Jericho fell. The Israelites were victorious.

The ease of that victory must have made Joshua overconfident. When the Israelites came to the next settlement, the tiny little town of Ai, Joshua forgot to seek the counsel of God. Instead, he sent some spies out to scout the town. The spies returned brimming with confidence. "Not all the army will have to go up against Ai," they said. "Send two or three thousand men to take it and do not weary the whole army, for only a few people live there" (Joshua 7:3).

Joshua sent a small force to conquer Ai—and the Israelites were clobbered and sent fleeing. Thirty-six Israelite soldiers were killed.

In anguish, Joshua prostrated himself before the Lord and asked, "Alas, Sovereign LORD, why did you ever bring this people across the Jordan to deliver us into the hands of the Amorites to destroy us?"

And God told Joshua to find someone who had stolen from the plunder of Jericho, in violation of God's command. "That is why the Israelites cannot stand against their enemies," God says. "They turn their backs and run because they have been made liable to destruction" (see Joshua 7:6-12).

Implied in God's words is a lesson for Joshua—and for us. He was telling Joshua, "If you had prayed, if you had sought my counsel, I would have told you there is sin in your camp. I would have warned you not to attack Ai until you had cleansed the people of this sin."

JOSHUA REPEATS HIS MISTAKE

I don't want to be too hard on Joshua. His decision to attack Ai without consulting God is a very human mistake. It's a mistake I've made again and again. I often attempt to do God's work in my own human wisdom and strength—and God has to knock me with a two-by-four to remind me of my own folly.

Unfortunately, Joshua didn't learn from his tragic mistake, as we see in Joshua 9. After the Israelites defeated Jericho and Ai, a nearby tribe called the Gibeonites feared for their lives. They knew God had commanded Israel to destroy the inhabitants of Canaan, so they devised a ruse to make a deceptive treaty with Joshua. They disguised themselves as travelers from a distant land, using old clothes, worn-out supplies, and stale food to make their story convincing. They told Joshua that they came from a far-off country and asked to make a peace treaty with Israel.

The Bible tells us, "The Israelites...did not inquire of the LORD" (Joshua 9:14). So once again, Joshua failed to seek God's guidance. He made a treaty with the Gibeonites, swearing by the Lord to let them live. Three days later, the Israelites discovered the deception. Even though he had been deceived, Joshua had to honor the treaty because of his oath before God.

The lessons of this story are as relevant today as they were so many centuries ago. The first lesson: Before making any important decision, always seek counsel from God. The second lesson: Don't let other people manipulate you with emotional sob stories. The Gibeonites claimed they had come from afar to learn about the God of Israel, but this was a lie—they had come from nearby to deceive the Israelites into making a peace treaty.

If you seek the wisdom that comes from God, he will help you see through the lies. He will keep you from being manipulated and deceived.

FIVE FATAL WORDS

We see a similar failure in the life of King David, who, according to the prophet Samuel, was a man after God's own heart (see 1 Samuel 13:14). If you know David's story well, you might find Samuel's words surprising. Though David truly was a man who hungered and thirsted for God and his righteousness, there was a time when David stopped being sober minded and vigilant. As a result, he ended up mired in lust, adultery, lies, betrayal, and even murder.

We find the story of David's moral failure in 2 Samuel 11 and 12. David's downfall begins with five fatal words at the end of 2 Samuel 11:1.

That verse tells us that, in the springtime, when kings go off to war, David sent his generals and his army out to wage war against the Ammonites. Then we read those five fatal words: "But David remained in Jerusalem."

David was not where he was supposed to be. He was not doing the job he was supposed to do. He did not exercise his primary responsibility as king of Israel. He paid no attention to Satan, who was prowling like a lion, seeking to devour him. He did not prepare himself for Satan's trap of temptation.

One evening, David had trouble sleeping. So he went out on the roof of the palace, and from the roof he saw a woman bathing.

Question: When you can't sleep, what do you do? Do you turn on the TV or scroll through Facebook or Instagram? I'm sure you don't go out and walk on your roof the way David did—but what you're doing could be just as harmful. Don't idle away the night, trying to become sleepy. Instead, try doing what I do when I have trouble sleeping. I have an audio version of the Bible by my bed. I can put an earbud in my ear and listen to the Word of God. Soon I fall deeply, blessedly asleep.

Every moment not dedicated to a godly purpose is an opportunity for Satan to steal his way into our lives. Had David chosen instead to pray or write songs to the Lord or study the Word of God, he would not have set in motion a series of events that would stain his reputation.

Instead, he went up on the rooftop, and he saw a woman who was another man's wife. Even then, he could have turned away—but no, he sent one of his servants to find out who the woman was. The servant returned and said, "She is Bathsheba, the daughter of Eliam and the wife of Uriah the Hittite."

He had started down the path of lust, and at every place where he might have repented and fled from sin, he kept going deeper and deeper, further and further. He told his servants to bring her to him. They did—

And David sinned with Bathsheba. Some weeks later, Bathsheba sent word to David: "I am pregnant."

You know the rest of the story—including how David tried to cover up his adultery with Bathsheba, how David tried to deceive his faithful, loyal soldier Uriah, and how when the deception failed, David resorted to cold-blooded, premeditated murder.

When Joshua was vigilant, he won battles, but when he let his guard down and failed to consult with the Lord, men died and battles were lost. When David was vigilant, he was a man after God's own heart, but when he let his guard down, he became an adulterer and a murderer.

That is why Peter, the great apostle, warns us, "Be alert and of sober mind. Your enemy the devil prowls around like a roaring lion looking for someone to devour."

DON'T LET GUILT AND SHAME KEEP YOU DOWN

Over the years, I've known many Christians who were trapped by feelings of discouragement and despondency. I don't mean people who are struggling with clinical depression or bipolar disorder or some other mental health issue. I'm referring to people who have normal mental health but who feel trapped by guilt, shame, or a sense of defeat they can't let go of.

Why can't they experience victory over those feelings? In most cases, I believe it's because they don't know how to repent. They don't know how to be renewed by the Holy Spirit. They don't know how to reclaim their rightful position and authority as children of the living God.

Judas's sin was no greater than Peter's. Judas betrayed Jesus—and Peter denied knowing Jesus after promising never to forsake him.

There's hardly a whit of difference between those two sins. But there is a world of difference between how each man dealt with his guilt and shame. Judas died in despair. Peter chose to repent and live for Jesus. Judas died in unbelief, rejecting the promise Jesus had made to rise from the dead. Peter lived in the faith that God accepts, renews, and reinstates repentant sinners.

It doesn't matter how great your sin. It doesn't matter how awful your shame. It doesn't matter how deep your failure. It doesn't matter how far you have fallen. Jesus wants to pick you up and put you back in his service.

But there is someone who wants to keep you down. His name is Satan, and he wants you to remain paralyzed by self-condemnation. He wants you to be so full of shame and self-loathing that you will always feel unworthy to serve Jesus.

In fact, the name "Satan" not only means *adversary* in Hebrew, but it also means *accuser*. That is why the book of Revelation calls Satan "the accuser of our brothers and sisters, who accuses them before our God day and night" (Revelation 12:10). Satan's goal is to accuse you continually, to make you feel guilty and ashamed, to convince you that your sins are beyond the reach of God's forgiveness and grace.

There is a very simple thing you can do that will defeat and frustrate Satan, that will fill him with impotent rage. All you have to do is get up, repent, receive God's forgiveness, and return to your love relationship with Jesus. That's it? Yes! That's it! If you do that one simple thing, you will deal Satan a crushing defeat!

That's what Peter did. He undoubtedly remembered the words of Jesus: "I have prayed for you, Simon, that your faith may not fail. And when you have turned back, strengthen your brothers." In other words, "After you repent, after you accept the mercy and forgiveness of God, after you are restored to spiritual sobriety—be a leader and strengthen your Christian brothers."

Peter carried out his mission. Not only did he lead the early church, but he also wrote two great letters, 1 and 2 Peter—letters that are brimming with wisdom and encouragement. Long after his martyrdom in Rome, Peter continued to strengthen millions of his Christian brothers and sisters with his Spirit-inspired words. He continues to strengthen you and me to this day.

Jesus said, "I give them eternal life, and they shall never perish; no one will snatch them out of my hand. My Father, who has given them to me, is greater than all; no one can snatch them out of my Father's hand" (John 10:28-29).

God has spoken, and Satan is powerless to change what God has decreed. But that doesn't mean Satan is completely powerless. If you stray from obedience to the Word of God, if you stray away from the protection of the Lord Jesus, you place yourself in extreme danger.

Your enemy prowls around, looking for someone to devour. Satan can devour your effectiveness for God. Satan can devour your peace of mind. Satan can devour your witness. Satan can devour your health. Satan can devour your marriage. Satan can devour your reputation. But he can only do these things *if you let him*. Don't leave an unlocked door for Satan to enter.

STUCK-IN-NEUTRAL CHRISTIANS

Every once in a while, I hear about a preacher or Christian author who dismisses the importance of spiritual warfare. They shrug off the reality of Satan. They roll their eyes at the mention of demonic activity.

According to them, Peter was an alarmist when he wrote, "Be alert and of sober mind." He should have written, "Relax! Chill out! Satan isn't a roaring lion—he's a paper tiger. Don't worry about him!"

And instead of urging us to put on the whole armor of God, Paul should have written, "You're saved. You checked that box. Your worries are over. As for the armor of God—leave it at home. You'll never need it."

There is a good reason why Peter and Paul did not write such things. They understood that Satan *does* have the ability to harm us—*if we let him*. That is why the New Testament tells us again and again to resist the devil, to be vigilant, and to armor ourselves for battle. Your enemy wants to keep you weak and vulnerable to attack, and that is why you must maintain a war footing, an aggressive stance toward Satan.

The vast majority of Christians live their lives in neutral gear. They aren't trying to move forward and take territory for the kingdom. They aren't trying to go in reverse and retreat from the foe. They are just idling in neutral, spiritually speaking. They are unproductive for the kingdom of God. They are saved, but their Christian walk is going nowhere.

Stuck-in-neutral Christians are profoundly satisfying to Satan. He loves seeing unproductive Christians. There are countless troops in God's army who have never gone through basic training, so they don't know that Jesus expects them to be taking territory in his name. One of Satan's proudest achievements is a Christian who is stuck in neutral.

If you've ever been in a car that was stuck in neutral, you know the feeling of pushing the accelerator, hearing the engine rev—but the car doesn't budge an inch. If you are a stuck-in-neutral Christian, you are just like that noisy, motionless car. It's time to take yourself out of neutral and put yourself in gear.

How do you do that?

You start with your personal spiritual disciplines—studying and meditating on God's Word, praying daily, and memorizing Scripture. Then you make sure you are involved with other believers, not just attending church on Sundays, but getting involved in a home Bible study and fellowship group.

Volunteer for outreach ministries in your church, such as ministries to the elderly, the homeless, or people in jails or prisons. Volunteer to serve in your church's food pantry or a crisis pregnancy center. And be ready, wherever you may be—at the office, on campus, in the neighborhood, in the waiting room—to share your faith with friends and strangers.

That's how you get your faith in gear. That's how you stop being stuck in neutral. That's how you start taking territory for the kingdom.

Satan doesn't want you to be roaring along life's highway, advancing the cause of Jesus wherever you go. He wants you to be stuck in the ditch alongside the road. He wants you to be obsessed with your annoyances and problems instead of sharing the good news of Jesus Christ. He wants to keep you focused on your tiny little kingdom so that you'll forget about the kingdom of God.

Stuck-in-neutral Christians are no threat to Satan. He leaves them alone. I urge you to report for duty and become a soldier of the army of God—a soldier on the front lines of the invisible war, a soldier who makes the devil tremble.

6

THE BLESSINGS OF SURRENDER

Jesus calls us to surrender. And those who surrender to Jesus can count on his promises—and his pardon. Surrendering to Jesus moves you from darkness to light, from the jungle of confusion to the sunlight of a new life. He said, "Take my yoke upon you and learn from me, for I am gentle and humble in heart, and you will find rest for your souls. For my yoke is easy and my burden is light" (Matthew 11:29-30).

THE BLESSINGS OF SURRENDER

In 1944, the Japanese Imperial Army deployed a platoon to the Philippine island of Lubang. The leader of the platoon was Lieutenant Hiroo Onoda. His commanders gave him strict orders to conduct guerrilla warfare, destroy the Lubang airfield and pier, gather intelligence, and above all, *never surrender*.

Onoda's superiors told him that Japan would never capitulate and that he must hold out at all costs. He must not be taken prisoner, and he was not permitted to take his own life. He must either accomplish his mission or die fighting. Onoda was radically committed to following orders. When Japan surrendered in August 1945, he refused to believe it—and he refused to surrender.

The government of Japan declared Onoda dead in 1959—but he was still alive. For nearly 30 years, Onoda and his slowly dwindling platoon of soldiers hid in the jungle, occasionally raiding local villagers, whom they mistook for enemy collaborators. They braved jungle snakes and stinging ants, surviving on a diet of wild bananas, wild coconuts, and rice that they seized on their raids.

When word reached the Japanese commanders that soldiers were still hiding out on Lubang, they sent planes to drop leaflets with information about Japan's surrender. But Lieutenant Onoda remembered the promise that his country would never capitulate, so he dismissed the leaflets as "Yankee propaganda."

For Lieutenant Hiroo Onoda, the war was still raging—and surrender was still unthinkable. He later reflected that he and his comrades had "developed so many fixed ideas that we were unable to understand anything that did not conform to them."

One by one, his companions either died or deserted. By 1974, Onoda was alone. His one-man war ended when a Japanese explorer, Norio Suzuki, tracked him down in the jungle. Even then, Onoda refused to surrender until Suzuki brought his former commanding officer to Lubang to formally relieve him of duty. When Suzuki returned with the commanding officer, Lieutenant Onoda surrendered. His war was finally over.

Onoda returned home to a hero's welcome—and to a world that was completely changed. His homeland had embraced peace and prosperity. The military cause he had clung to had long since faded into history. He knew at last that his 30 years of struggle under harsh and primitive conditions had been in vain.[1]

Before he surrendered, Lieutenant Onoda was isolated from reality. After he surrendered, he was finally able to heal, to understand the real world, and to recover from his long ordeal. Surrender brought him peace. Surrender showed him the truth. Surrender gave him a new beginning.

The blessings of surrender come to those who stop resisting and struggling—and who trade in their delusions for truth and reality.

SURRENDERING TO JESUS

Jesus calls us to surrender. And those who surrender to Jesus can count on his promises—and his pardon. Surrendering to Jesus moves you from darkness to light, from the jungle of confusion to the sunlight of a new life. He said, "Take my yoke upon you and learn from me, for I am gentle and humble in heart, and you will find rest for your souls. For my yoke is easy and my burden is light" (Matthew 11:29-30).

A yoke is a harness a farmer places on a beast of burden so that he can control the animal. You cannot wear the yoke Jesus places on you unless you completely surrender to him. Surrendering to Jesus is not merely a matter of relinquishing our possessions, our pride, or our status. Surrender must include a complete surrender of our will to the control of the Lord Jesus.

Throughout his ministry, Jesus called people to lay down their pride, self-will, and worldly attachments in order to receive abundant life in him. One of the people Jesus called was a Roman centurion—a soldier in the Roman occupation army. Despite his position of authority, the centurion approached Jesus not with demands but with faith. He believed that Jesus could heal his servant with just a word.

The centurion said, "Lord, I do not deserve to have you come under my roof. But just say the word, and my servant will be healed" (Matthew 8:8). The centurion's surrender to Jesus involved a complete trust in Jesus's authority and power. Jesus marveled at his faith, declaring it greater than any he had found in Israel.

In Luke 7, we find another story of surrender to Jesus. A woman entered the home of Simon the Pharisee where Jesus was having dinner. Luke describes her as a woman who had "lived a sinful life." She brought with her an alabaster jar of perfume, her most prized possession—a jar that symbolizes the beauty of surrender exemplified in repentance and devotion. She poured the costly perfume on the feet of Jesus, weeping as she anointed him, and drying his feet with her hair. The people around the room eyed her with scorn, but she didn't care what anyone thought of her. Nothing mattered to her but this act of surrender and selfless devotion.

When Simon the Pharisee criticized the woman, Jesus turned to him and said, "I came into your house. You did not give me any water for my feet, but she wet my feet with her tears and wiped them with her hair. You did not give me a kiss, but this woman, from the time I entered, has not stopped kissing my feet. You did not put oil on my head, but she has poured perfume on my feet. Therefore, I tell you, her many sins have been forgiven—as her great love has shown. But whoever has been forgiven little loves little." Then he turned to the woman and said, "Your sins are forgiven…Your faith has saved you; go in peace" (Luke 7:36-50).

This woman's story reminds us of the beauty of surrender—the beauty of sacrificing everything, of setting aside our pride, and of giving ourselves completely to Jesus in repentance, gratitude, and worship. If you and I were in the physical presence of Jesus right now, who would we most identify with—the woman with the jar of perfume or Simon the Pharisee?

The most dramatic example of surrender to Jesus was the conversion of the apostle Paul. As a fanatical persecutor of Christians, Paul encountered the risen Lord on the road to Damascus. A light from heaven flashed around him, and he heard a voice call him by name and ask, "Why do you persecute me?" (Acts 9:4). From that day forward, Paul's life was completely changed—and completely surrendered to Jesus. He let go of his status, ambition, and misguided zeal in order to proclaim the very gospel he had once opposed. Paul's surrender was total; he described his life as being "crucified with Christ," no longer living for himself but for the one who had saved him (Galatians 2:20). His transformation proves that radical conversion can change anyone, even the most hardened enemies of Jesus.

In contrast to these three examples of surrender to Jesus, we find the story of the rich young ruler in Matthew 19. When Jesus invited this eager young man to sell his possessions and follow him, the young man refused to surrender. Instead, he walked away from Jesus. Though he was sorrowful, though he truly wanted to follow Jesus, he was unwilling to part with his wealth (Matthew 19:22). He clung to his earthly security, unable to embrace the eternal treasure Jesus offered. Surrender requires that we let go of whatever stands between us and Jesus, whether it is self-will, pride, or possessions.

In these examples, we see that surrendering to Jesus is not about losing—it's about gaining. The centurion gained the healing he sought, the woman with the alabaster jar received forgiveness and peace, and Paul became the greatest missionary of the early church. In contrast, the rich young ruler left with nothing but sorrow. The choice to surrender may seem costly, but it really costs us nothing of lasting value, and it opens the door to true blessing, purpose, and abundant life in Jesus.

GOD BEGINS WITH WHAT YOU HAVE

God always begins with what you have. The woman who anointed the feet of Jesus had one thing—an alabaster jar of perfume. She had nothing else to offer Jesus—unless you count her tears of remorse and her hair, with which she dried his feet. She had no pride, no position, no reputation.

She had a heart full of love and gratitude—and she freely surrendered that to Jesus. She had tears of remorse and kisses of affection—and she lavished them on the feet of Jesus. And because she offered him what little she had, sacrificing even her most precious possession, Jesus said to her, "Your faith has saved you; go in peace."

If God is not blessing your life, there is a reason for that. If God is not answering your prayers, there is a reason for that. If God is not sending revival into your life, into your family, into your church, into your nation, there is a reason for that. Why is there turmoil in our streets, in our churches, in our lives today? It's because we are holding out on God. We are not surrendering to him. We are not letting God have his way in our lives.

The Word of God tells us why he is not sending a revival. The Bible tells us why we are in a state of spiritual depression as a nation. God will not send a revival into the lives of disobedient Christians. He will never send revival to unsurrendered people. He will not bless us if we have unyielding hearts.

Some people think that if we gather thousands of Christians under one roof and call upon God and pray for revival, then revival will come. But God says that is not true:

> Your New Moon feasts and your appointed festivals
> > I hate with all my being.
> They have become a burden to me;
> > I am weary of bearing them.
> When you spread out your hands in prayer,
> > I hide my eyes from you;
> even when you offer many prayers,
> > I am not listening (Isaiah 1:14-15).

God will not bring revival to unsurrendered people. He will not listen to the prayers of people who live in disobedience. There is no use praying to God when we keep cherished sins in our lives. The prayers and religious rituals of those who hold out on God are wearying to him.

Take, for example, giving to God. The Bible tells us that the tithe belongs to God. "A tithe of everything from the land, whether grain from the soil or fruit from the trees, belongs to the Lord; it is holy to the Lord" (Leviticus 27:30). The tithe is not yours, it's not mine, it's the Lord's. In Malachi 3, God says to his people:

"Will a mere mortal rob God? Yet you rob me.

"But you ask, 'How are we robbing you?'

"In tithes and offerings. You are under a curse—your whole nation—because you are robbing me. Bring the whole tithe into the storehouse, that there may be food in my house. Test me in this," says the LORD Almighty, "and see if I will not throw open the floodgates of heaven and pour out so much blessing that there will not be room enough to store it" (Malachi 3:8-10).

Many Christians today are living in stolen homes, driving to church in stolen cars, wearing stolen clothes, and buying meals with stolen money. God's message to those Christians is clear: "You are robbing me. Bring the whole tithe into the storehouse."

WHAT ARE YOU HOLDING BACK?

I guarantee that when the woman poured her precious perfume onto the feet of Jesus, she was giving much more than a tithe. She was surrendering to Jesus the most precious thing she owned. She came clean with Jesus. She emptied her pockets with Jesus. She held nothing back. And Jesus blessed her for it.

Do you want God's power to fight the battles and skirmishes of the invisible war? Do you want the floodgates of heaven to open wide and pour vast blessings into your life? Then you must come clean with God. Do you want to see your prayers answered? He will not bless you until you stop holding out on him. God doesn't need your money or your possessions—but you need to surrender them.

Please understand. I'm not saying that surrendering everything to God means that he will immediately answer all your prayers. God is sovereign, and he has purposes for delaying that we cannot understand. No one was ever more completely surrendered to God than the apostle Paul. He asked God in prayer to remove this "thorn in my flesh" (a physical ailment), yet God chose not to answer that prayer (see 2 Corinthians 12:6-10).

Prayer is not a vending machine. You can't deposit a surrendered heart and expect God's answer to pop out of the machine. At the same time, if God is not answering your prayers, it may well be that you are holding something back from God. So it's wise to search your heart and make sure nothing is hindering God's power from being unleashed in your life.

What are you holding back from God? Your prized possessions? Your acts of service and worship to Jesus? Your tears of remorse and gratitude? God will only bless you to the extent that you are surrendered to him. If you hold back a certain part of your life from God, he cannot bless that part of your life. What do you think will happen when you say, "God, you can get into this area in my life, but I'm maintaining control of this other area—that's mine, God, not yours"? If that is your attitude, then you have blocked God's ability to bless that part of your life.

Surrender to God any resentment or anger you harbor in your heart. The Holy Spirit cannot pour blessings into a heart filled with bitterness.

Surrender to God your critical spirit, your arrogant opinions, your desire to control, your "me first" attitude. The Holy Spirit cannot make you more Christlike if you continually insist on having your own way.

Surrender to God your greed, covetousness, and materialism—your desire to amass treasures and worldly security on Earth. The Holy Spirit cannot fill you with the blessings of heaven while your heart is set on worldly things.

Surrender to God your spirit of gossip, your spirit of murmuring and dissension, your jealousy over the success of others. The Spirit of Unity cannot fill you with his peace while you stir up conflict and opposition.

Surrender to God your spirit of lust and sexual immorality. The Holy Spirit cannot fill you with the purity of God while your mind is clouded with thoughts of sin.

Surrender even your right to self-defense.

I remember one occasion where someone said false things about me, and I wanted *so badly* to lash back and defend myself from the accusations. But I felt the Lord saying to me, "Don't say a word." Oh, that was hard! It was killing me! I said to the Lord, "But what if people believe it? What if my reputation is harmed?" But the Lord kept saying, "Don't say a word." So, reluctantly, I surrendered my right to self-defense. About two years after that, the truth came out—and the Lord vindicated me. I'm glad I didn't defend myself—but it was a hard lesson to learn.

It saddens me deeply to see a believer who has ceased to be an empty vessel for the Spirit of God to fill. Many believers have clung to bad habits, bad attitudes, bad goals, bad character traits, and sinful desires for so long that the Holy Spirit no longer tries to pour his blessings into their lives—and they don't even realize it!

Many in the church today are just faking it—going through the motions and doing and saying what is expected of them in the Christian culture. That is not honoring to God. He doesn't care what people think of you. What's vitally, eternally important is what God thinks of you. I urge you to surrender yourself completely and offer yourself to God as an empty jar, ready to be filled by the Holy Spirit.

If you want the Spirit of God to be poured into your life, into your family, into your church, into your nation, surrender yourself completely to God. Don't wait another day. Surrender now and watch how he blesses you, how he answers your prayers, how he empowers you to withstand and fend off the attacks of Satan.

SURRENDERING THROUGH PRAYER

God is more eager to pour his blessings and his Spirit upon you than you are willing to receive. In fact, it is amazing to me that we are often so reluctant to receive his blessings out of fear that he will change us in ways we won't like, or send us someplace we won't like, or deprive us of something we cherish. We can't imagine the joys and blessings he wants to shower upon us—so we resist him and hold back areas of our lives from him.

That is why we need to go to God in prayer, asking him to align our will with his will. That is why we need to spend time with him every day, surrendering ourselves to him again and again and again. Surrender is not a once-and-for-all act. It's a process that must be renewed daily.

I suggest you begin each morning with a time of refreshment from Scripture and prayer with the Father. Here are some passages that are especially appropriate for your morning prayer times:

- "Let the morning bring me word of your unfailing love, for I have put my trust in you. Show me the way I should go, for to you I entrust my life" (Psalm 143:8).

- "Hear my cry for help, my King and my God, for to you I pray. In the morning, LORD, you hear my voice; in the morning I lay my requests before you and wait expectantly" (Psalm 5:2-3).

- "May these words of my mouth and this meditation of my heart be pleasing in your sight, LORD, my Rock and my Redeemer" (Psalm 19:14).

- "Guide me in your truth and teach me, for you are God my Savior, and my hope is in you all day long" (Psalm 25:5).

The place to renew our commitment to complete surrender to God is in our "prayer closet." I'm not saying you literally need to pray in a closet of your house, but I do encourage you to find a private place where you can pray without any hindrances, distractions, or inhibitions.

Jesus said, "When you pray, go into your room, close the door and pray to your Father, who is unseen. Then your Father, who sees what is done in secret, will reward you" (Matthew 6:6). Jesus is giving us the same prayer advice that he himself followed. As the Gospel of Luke tells us, "But Jesus often withdrew to lonely places and prayed" (Luke 5:16).

If possible, find a place where you can pray out loud to God, a place where no one else can hear you. When you pray silently, your praying can easily turn into distracted thinking. Praying aloud helps to keep you focused on your connection to God.

Go into your sanctuary of prayer and shut out all worry and fear, all cynicism and worldliness, all busyness and distraction. Turn off your phone and other devices. It's hard to hear the still, small voice of the Spirit over all the other voices clamoring for your attention. Create a safe, quiet space where you can get down to business with God. And trust me on this: God wants to give to you more generously than you are able to receive.

Shut the door and pray so that God can bless you. Jesus said, "If you then, though you are evil, know how to give good gifts to your children, how much more will your Father in heaven give the Holy Spirit to those who ask him!" (Luke 11:13).

Make a daily commitment that your head will not touch your pillow at night until you have spent significant time in prayer. Keep a prayer journal. Fill it with inspiring Scripture passages. Keep a list of people and concerns to pray for. When you tell someone, "I'll pray for you," write down their name and their need in your prayer journal. Check in with them from time to time—and experience the joy of hearing that your prayers are being answered.

You may want to begin your prayer time with the prayer that Jesus taught his disciples, the Lord's Prayer. You remember how it begins: "Our Father in heaven, hallowed be your name, your kingdom come, your will be done, on earth as it is in heaven" (Matthew 6:9-10).

If you are sincere about wanting to surrender your life and your will to God, I have a suggestion. When you pray the Lord's Prayer, add these words: "in my life." Pray, "Father in heaven, hallowed be your name *in my life*, your kingdom come *in my life*, your will be done *in my life*." Pray every day for God to make his name holy through your life, to bring his kingdom into reality through your life, and to align your will with his perfect will. Pray this prayer every day and see if it doesn't produce profound changes in your attitude and your will.

Pray also for wisdom to see through Satan's lies and tactics. Pray for strength to resist the devil's attacks and overcome his deception.

Pray for the people in your life who are deceived by Satan and by the delusions and ideologies of this dying world. As Paul said, "The god of this age has blinded the minds of unbelievers, so that they cannot see the light of the gospel that displays the glory of Christ, who is the image of God" (2 Corinthians 4:4).

Ask God to reveal to you any areas of your life where you are putting worldly values or your own selfish wants ahead of his will for your life. Ask God to search your mind and heart, and to reveal any places in your life where you have left a back door unlocked—a place where the enemy might enter and gain access to your life.

If you feel that the enemy is attacking you in any area of your life, lift it up to God in prayer. Surrender that area of your life to God.

Ask him for protection. Ask him to take control. Ask him to fight for you. Ask him to be your strength. Ask him to give you the victory.

Remember that Satan has already been defeated by the cross of Jesus. Fear and death have been conquered by the empty tomb of Jesus. Satanic delusion and spiritual darkness have been shattered and scattered by the good news of Jesus. Surrender to Jesus through prayer, and see God win victory after victory in your spiritual battles.

THE WAY TO VICTORY

A.W. Tozer has described the Christian life as a pathway of paradoxes and contradictions. In an essay called "That Incredible Christian," he writes:

> The Christian believes that in Christ he has died, yet he is more alive than before and he fully expects to live forever. He walks on earth while seated in heaven and though born on earth he finds that after his conversion he is not at home here...
>
> He loses his life to save it and is in danger of losing it if he attempts to preserve it. He goes down to get up. If he refuses to go down, he is already down, but when he starts down, he is on his way up.
>
> He is strongest when he is weakest and weakest when he is strong. Though poor he has the power to make others rich, but when he becomes rich his ability to enrich others vanishes. He has most after he has given most away and has least when he possesses most...
>
> He fears God but is not afraid of Him. In God's presence he feels overwhelmed and undone, yet there is nowhere

he would rather be than in that presence. He knows that he has been cleansed from his sin, yet he is painfully conscious that in his flesh dwells no good thing.[2]

Clearly, the Christian life is rich in paradoxes and spiritual ironies. I would add one more paradox to Tozer's list: Christians believe that the key to spiritual victory is surrender.

Never underestimate God. There is no limit to what his power can accomplish through you *if* you're completely surrendered to him. It doesn't matter how insignificant and inadequate you feel, how weak and poor you are. He will mend your brokenness with his strength. He will supply everything you lack through his infinite riches and resources. The only thing that can keep him from pouring his infinite blessings into your life is if you hold back your will, if you retain control.

Surrender, surrender! That is the way to victory in the invisible war.

God will always make ample provision for his people to overcome the enemy. Jesus promised that the gates of hell could not and would not prevail against his church. Whatever you lack, he will provide—and when he provides, his provision always satisfies.

Are you wounded? He is the balm. Are you sick? He is the medicine. Are you poor? He is your limitless wealth. Are you hungry? He is the Bread of Life. Are you thirsty? He is the Living Water. Are you in debt? He forgives all of our debts. Are you condemned? He is your pardon. Are you facing a storm? He is your anchor. Are you in darkness? He is the Light.

God is not honored by the masks we wear on Sunday mornings. He is not honored by the "Christianese" dialect we speak at church. He is not honored when our Sunday morning selves are different from our Monday-through-Saturday selves. God is honored by our obedience and our complete surrender to him. God is honored when we stop holding out on him and start yielding everything to him.

God is not impressed with who we are. He is not impressed with our accomplishments, our titles, our degrees, or our accolades. When the Roman centurion approached Jesus and asked him to heal his servant, Jesus was not impressed by this Roman officer's title or authority or position in the Roman army—but Jesus was very impressed with his faith.

When a persecutor of the church named Saul was stricken by his encounter with Jesus on the road to Damascus, Jesus was not impressed by his years of education or his powerful position as a Pharisee—but Jesus was very impressed with his complete surrender as the apostle Paul.

God is only impressed by our faith and our total surrender to him. Our sincere prayer must be, "Lord, I come to you in abject surrender. There are things I'm struggling to give over to you, but I ask you to help me surrender them to you. I cannot do this in my strength, so please give me your strength so that I can surrender all."

TAKE THE BATTLE SERIOUSLY

I've heard some Christians trivialize the invisible war by treating every little problem as an attack from the enemy: "I can't find my car keys—I'm being attacked by Satan!" "My knee is sore—it's an attack of the devil!" Not every problem in life is a spiritual battle. Sometimes misplaced car keys or a sore knee simply are what they are, nothing more.

People who claim every minor trial is an attack by the enemy are really preoccupied with themselves. Satan has more important things to do than hide your keys or afflict your joints. The Bible teaches us that the one thing the enemy does attack viciously is the preaching of the gospel of Jesus Christ. The one thing that infuriates Satan to no end is when souls are saved and snatched from his clutches. The one thing that Satan will ruthlessly attack is a life that is completely surrendered to Jesus Christ.

God is ultimately victorious. No one can defeat God. No one can defeat the plans and purposes of God, no matter how hard they try. The Old Testament prophet Jonah tried to thwart God's purpose and run from the presence of God—but when a storm landed him in the belly of a big fish, he learned that God's plan cannot be thwarted. After the fish vomited him up onto the shore, Jonah went on to carry out the plan of God.

Because God cannot be defeated, doesn't it make sense to surrender completely to the winning side? Yes, it is scary to follow Jesus in the adventure of faith. The invisible war is a *real* war, even though we can't see it raging. But thanks be to God, he gives us the courage we need to fight on. He encourages every man, woman, and child who is fully surrendered to him.

The greater the battle, the more triumphant the victory. The fiercer the opposition, the sweeter the conquest. The more vicious the attack, the deeper our experience of Jesus our Commander, fighting on our behalf. As Hudson Taylor, a pioneering missionary to China, once wrote, "God's power is available power. We are a supernatural people, born-again by a supernatural birth, kept by a supernatural power, sustained on supernatural food, taught by a supernatural Teacher, from a supernatural Book. We are led by a supernatural Captain in right paths to assured victories."[3]

I believe our supernatural Captain expects much of us, especially of Christians in North America. Jesus said, "From everyone who has been given much, much will be demanded; and from the one who has been entrusted with much, much more will be asked" (Luke 12:48).

For decades, all across America, there have been as many churches on street corners as gas stations. The Word of God has been preached on radio and television, and proclaimed in books by the carload. Because so much biblical truth has been entrusted to us, I believe

Jesus is expecting more from us than just a little church attendance once a week.

You might say, "Well, what can I do? I don't have the gift of evangelism." Maybe not—but every believer has a testimony to share, a story that begins, "Let me tell you what God has done for me…" You don't have to preach like Billy Graham. Just tell the simple story of what Jesus has done in your life.

God gives the spiritual gift of evangelism to some, and he gives other gifts to other believers. But every believer has at least one spiritual gift. What gift has God given to you? Do you have the gift of prayer? When was the last time you interceded for the lost? Do you have the gift of giving? Then give generously to reaching the lost. Do you have the gift of mercy? The gift of hospitality? Whatever gift God has given you, use it to the utmost to serve Jesus and his kingdom.

It doesn't take eloquence to share the good news of Jesus Christ. It just takes the surrender of your will. I have a friend, a prominent businessman, who is always ready to share Christ with the people he meets. He's not a theologian. He's not a preacher. He has a very simple message. He will sit with you and say, "Let me ask you something. Would you let your son die on a cross for a rascal?" People always answer, "No." Then he'll say, "But that's exactly what God did for me."

It's such a simple message, yet it is so profound. It's the whole gospel in a few sentences. I hope my friend's example will challenge you to find ways to share the gospel of Jesus Christ with your neighbors and relatives, your coworkers and classmates. All it takes is your willingness to surrender to Jesus and pray, "Lord Jesus, give me the courage to speak up and give me your words to speak." Jesus will grab your hand and hold it tightly as you give your simple testimony of faith in Jesus.

William Booth, the founder of the Salvation Army, did many great things in the name of Jesus Christ, but his life of service to God began with a decision he made when he was just 15 years old. It was then that he attended a chapel service and heard the good news of Jesus Christ. He was so profoundly impacted by the gospel that he immediately surrendered his life to Jesus. Afterward, he wrote in his journal, "God shall have all there is of William Booth."

In 1865, Booth founded the Christian Mission in London. He developed a strategy of preaching the gospel while providing food, housing, and services to the poor and marginalized people of the streets of London. All were welcomed with the love of Christ—including alcoholics, addicts, felons, and prostitutes.

Thirteen years later, in 1878, Booth renamed the mission "the Salvation Army," and he gave the new organization a military structure with army-style ranks. As the Salvation Army became more well known, it soon faced opposition. Hecklers tried to disrupt Salvation Army meetings. Booth and others in the organization were sometimes harassed and fined by the city officials. It was spiritual warfare, and Booth refused to back down. "We are a salvation people," he said. "This is our specialty—getting saved and keeping saved, and then getting somebody else saved."

On August 20, 1912, William Booth died at age 83. His memorial service was attended by about 35,000 people, including representatives of the King and Queen of England. *The War Cry*, the publication of the Salvation Army, declared, "The old warrior finally laid down his sword."

He had fought hard in the invisible war, and the organization he founded continues its work around the world today, spreading the gospel while fighting poverty and addiction. His long fight ended as it began—not with a declaration of war, but with a statement of total, unconditional surrender: "God shall have all there is of William Booth."[4]

May it be said that God shall have all there is of you and me as well. May we finish our fight as William Booth finished his—showered by the blessings of surrender.

7

KNOW YOUR ENEMY

Unless we are constantly alert to the enemy's deception, we'll fall for it. That's why Paul warns us to be informed and vigilant, "in order that Satan might not outwit us. For we are not unaware of his schemes" (2 Corinthians 2:11). We must be like experienced detectives who know that one of the keys to solving crimes is to study the personality profile of the criminal. We need to understand the criminal mind, the criminal character, the criminal modus operandi.

KNOW YOUR ENEMY

A personality profile is a summary of a person's unique traits and tendencies. One famous example of a personality profile is the Myers-Briggs Type Indicator (MBTI), which uses a self-reporting questionnaire to categorize individuals according to four dichotomies—Introversion versus Extraversion, Sensing versus Intuition, Thinking versus Feeling, and Judging versus Perceiving. If you ever hear someone say, "I'm an ENTP" or "She's an ISFJ," those comments are based on the Myers-Briggs test.

Now, I don't think Satan has ever taken the Myers-Briggs personality profile, and I doubt he'd answer the questions honestly if he did. But we don't need a test to tell us just what kind of creature Satan is or how he thinks. We have plenty of evidence of Satan's behavior in the record of history.

We know he is a deceiver—and we know that the deceptions of Satan have caused misery and destruction since the beginning of time. Deception is Satan's greatest weapon. The Bible tells us that one day we will see his destruction: "The great dragon was hurled down—that ancient serpent called the devil, or Satan, who leads the whole world astray. He was hurled to the earth, and his angels with him" (Revelation 12:9).

The destruction of Satan is something to look forward to. In the meantime, Satan continues to lead the whole world astray. He even leads entire churches astray. The landscape is strewn with once-believing churches that have abandoned faith in God. I could list for you dozens of once-believing pastors who have now turned their backs on the faith. There are dozens of formerly Christian colleges and universities that used to honor Jesus but are now indoctrination factories for godless ideologies. They were seduced and led astray by Satan the deceiver.

Satan works overtime on Christian leaders, pastors, elders, teachers, school principals, university presidents, and professors. He attacks leaders so that, through the leaders, he can multiply his influence on the followers. He attacks shepherds so that he can render the sheep vulnerable to his predatory raids.

Unless we are constantly alert to the enemy's deception, we'll fall for it. That's why Paul warns us to be informed and vigilant, "in order that Satan might not outwit us. For we are not unaware of his schemes" (2 Corinthians 2:11). We must be like experienced detectives who know that one of the keys to solving crimes is to study the personality profile of the criminal. We need to understand the criminal mind, the criminal character, the criminal modus operandi.

In this chapter, we will examine Satan's personality profile. We will undertake a sevenfold study of Satan's behavior so that we can be prepared to recognize him—and defeat him through the power of the Holy Spirit.

1. SATAN'S SCHEME: QUESTION AUTHORITY

The first point of Satan's seven-point personality profile is: *Question authority*. Satan and his demons continually tempt us to question authority—especially God's authority and the authority of the Word of God. Today, the Bible is even being questioned by pastors in evangelical churches.

Satan also wants children and young people to question their parents' authority. I don't think it's an accident that, just a few verses before Paul talks about spiritual warfare in Ephesians 6, he writes, "Children, obey your parents in the Lord, for this is right. 'Honor your father and mother'—which is the first commandment with a promise—'so that it may go well with you and that you may enjoy long life on the earth'" (Ephesians 6:1-3). One of Satan's schemes is to break down parental authority and our children's respect for that authority.

I had two uncles who died in World War II, before I was born. They were my mother's older brothers, and she often talked about them. They died fighting against the Axis forces of Nazi Germany and Italy in the Battles of El Alamein in 1942. There were two battles, one in July, another in October–November, and they took place in the western desert of Egypt, near the Mediterranean coast.

Because these battles took place in the land of my birth, we studied them in school. The Allied forces—the Americans and the British—were continually outmaneuvered by the Nazi general Erwin Rommel, who was nicknamed "the Desert Fox." British prime minister Winston Churchill knew that the Allied forces outnumbered Nazi Germany's, yet the Germans repeatedly outfought the Allies. So Churchill sent his most brilliant tactician, Field Marshal Bernard Montgomery, to North Africa. Known for his autocratic leadership style and his tactical brilliance, Montgomery was determined to find out the reason for the Allied losses.

I learned in school that Montgomery quickly discovered that whenever a decision was handed down by the generals, people in the ranks would question and criticize and argue with that decision. The result was that the Allied fighting force, though superior to the Nazis in every way, was paralyzed by disagreement. Montgomery decided that this dissension was the reason for the Allies' defeats. He immediately put an end to the questioning of orders. Soon after that, Montgomery's forces cornered the Nazis, and Rommel was forced to retreat.

When Lucifer challenged God's authority, he was thrown out of heaven—and he wants to lure the followers of Jesus to the same fate. Satan wants Christians to be paralyzed and defeated, just like the Allied forces in Egypt were.

Satan used the same strategy with Adam and Eve in the garden. He didn't come to Eve and say, "Follow me, obey me, and you can spend eternity in the lake of fire with me." No, that's not how Satan operates. His scheme is to slyly plant questions about God's authority in the minds of his victims.

The Genesis account begins, "The serpent was more crafty than any of the wild animals the LORD God had made. He said to the woman, 'Did God really say, "You must not eat from any tree in the garden"?'" (Genesis 3:1).

Satan used the serpent as his mouthpiece to break down Eve's defenses. He didn't come right out and accuse God of lying. He just asked her a "leading question"—a question designed to lead Eve to the conclusion he wanted.

In all the centuries since then, Satan's strategy has never changed. He turns a command from the Word of God into a debate. Did God *really* say it this way? Are you *sure* you heard God correctly? Are you *certain* that's what God meant?

We hear that same line of questioning all the time today: Is this biblical command still relevant in the twenty-first century? We have so much more knowledge now than people had back then. Are you sure that this verse or that command is *really* what God means today?

Without making any direct accusation against God, Satan planted doubt in Eve's mind. He prompted Eve to debate within her own mind what God had commanded. Satan still uses this technique against us today. I've seen it again and again, as denomination after denomination, church after church, family after family becomes embroiled in that ancient debate: "Did God really say…?" Many churches and individual believers have fallen for Satan's scheme.

If Satan can get you to debate an issue that has been settled in the Word of God, he is two-thirds of the way to victory. If he can get you to question the authority of Scripture when it comes to political questions, social questions, and moral questions—sex outside of marriage or abortion or euthanasia or so-called "transgender rights"—he's got you right where he wants you. If he can get you to accept the popular myth that "God doesn't care what you do, as long as you are happy," Satan can pull your strings.

We are all tempted. But when we are tempted, God will pour out his power on us if we place our complete trust in him and his Word. He will keep us alert to Satan's schemes—and he will give us the victory.

2. SATAN'S SUBTLETY: ATTEND CHURCH

Satan does not attack churches; he infiltrates them. Through his many demonic agents in the world, Satan has already moved into many churches. He has introduced his lies and deceptive standards to many congregations. He has turned falsehood into gospel. He has dispatched his human emissaries and placed them in leadership positions in churches.

The most dangerous lie is a lie that closely resembles the truth. And Satan's most dangerous deceivers are those who most closely resemble believers. It was Vance Havner who observed, "Satan is not fighting churches; he is joining them. He does more harm by sowing tares than by pulling up wheat. He accomplishes more by imitation than by outright opposition."[1]

Paul confronted Satan's infiltration of the church from the very outset. He wrote to the churches in Galatia: "I am astonished that you are so quickly deserting the one who called you to live in the grace of Christ and are turning to a different gospel—which is really no gospel at all. Evidently some people are throwing you into confusion and are trying to pervert the gospel of Christ" (Galatians 1:6-7).

False Christians had joined the Galatian church and were promoting a false gospel—a perverted version of the true gospel. These deceptive teachers spread a false doctrine which added legalistic requirements to the gospel. Instead of preaching that salvation is by grace through faith in Christ alone, these teachers taught the Galatians that they needed to follow the Jewish laws regarding circumcision and dietary restrictions. These teachings undermined the gospel of grace and salvation through faith in Jesus Christ.

There are still false teachers infiltrating the church today. They tell us that Jesus was a great moral teacher, and if he were among us today, teaching and preaching, he would be an advocate for the transgender movement and "queerness," he would tell us that the Bible is a "living document" that we should reinterpret according to the latest social and political fads, that love and compassion are more important than morality and righteousness, and that "saving the planet" is more important than saving souls.

Satan has joined the church, and he is spreading confusion and falsehood. The only antidote to Satan's lies is the truth of God's authoritative Word. What God told ancient Israel is still essential instruction for us today: "And now, Israel, what does the LORD your God ask of you but to fear the LORD your God, to walk in obedience to him, to love him, to serve the LORD your God with all your heart and with all your soul, and to observe the LORD's commands and decrees that I am giving you today for your own good?" (Deuteronomy 10:12-13).

Jesus expects us to hold fast to his truth. As he said in the Sermon on the Mount, "Anyone who sets aside one of the least of these commands and teaches others accordingly will be called least in the kingdom of heaven, but whoever practices and teaches these commands will be called great in the kingdom of heaven" (Matthew 5:19).

If anyone in your church preaches or teaches anything that is opposed to Scripture, that deviates from Scripture, or that sets aside the commands of God, then you know that your church has been infiltrated. Satan has come to church. Don't listen to false teachers. Don't allow yourself to be infected by their lies.

Remember what Jesus said: "If you hold to my teaching, you are really my disciples. Then you will know the truth, and the truth will set you free" (John 8:31-32).

3. SATAN'S SCENARIO: PRETEND TO BE SYMPATHETIC

Satan pretends to be oh-so-sympathetic. He will listen to your complaints, and he'll offer you his soothing comfort—and his false solutions to your problems. Satan's tactics often involve blending truth with lies, appealing to human weaknesses, and feigning concern for people's well-being. He will prey on your emotions, exploiting your doubts and vulnerabilities to lead you astray.

In Genesis, Satan engages Eve in a conversation and pretends to be sympathetic to her because of the limits God has imposed. He questions God's command and implies that God is withholding something good from her. This feigned concern for Eve's rights and freedom deceives her into disobedience.

In Luke 4, Satan comes to Jesus in the wilderness, pretending to be sympathetic to Jesus's hunger. "If you are the Son of God," Satan says, "tell this stone to become bread" (Luke 4:3). Though Satan pretends to be sympathetic to Jesus's plight, he is really trying to undermine God's plan to redeem the human race.

Satan's pretended sympathy for our problems is one of the ways he disguises himself "as an angel of light" (2 Corinthians 11:14). For example, many people, feeling confused about their gender identity, feeling they don't quite fit into society, find their way into the LGBTQ+ culture. There, they find sympathy for their hurt and confusion. People tell them that society is to blame, or the church is to blame, for their problems. They say, "You were assigned the wrong gender at birth, but if you'll simply have an experimental, mutilating medical procedure, all your problems will be solved." This is one of Satan's most destructive lies.

How many times have you heard someone say, "I have to find a church that meets my needs"? This attitude is rooted in a satanic deception. It is rooted in the notion that the church exists to meet your needs. And no church, no Bible teacher, no ministry can ever truly meet your needs. The church exists to bring you to Jesus—and *he* will meet your needs.

Jesus said, "So do not worry, saying, 'What shall we eat?' or 'What shall we drink?' or 'What shall we wear?' For the pagans run after all these things, and your heavenly Father knows that you need them. But seek first his kingdom and his righteousness, and all these things will be given to you as well" (Matthew 6:31-33).

It's the pagans, Jesus said, who constantly worry about having their needs met. But Christians are commanded to seek God's kingdom and God's righteousness—which means we should stop worrying about our "needs." If we do this, then all our needs will be met.

Many churches market themselves as the place where your needs will be met. This is how many churches fall into Satan's trap. When a church begins to center itself around meeting felt needs, it soon forgets that the true center of the church is God and his Word. Empathy for hurting, needy people is a good thing, and Jesus encourages us to care for people in need. But Satan loves to get us sidetracked on *good* things so that we neglect the *best* thing, the *essential* thing, which is Jesus and the Word.

A church that makes "felt needs" the center of its mission will soon find that it has lost its love for Jesus. But a church that loves Jesus and obeys his Word will naturally be a congregation that meets people's needs.

4. SATAN'S SHAM: BE A MASTER FORGER

Before he rebelled and fell, Satan lived and served in the throne room of God. He knows the voice of God—and he can imitate God's voice. He knows what the light of heaven looks like—and he can appear as an angel of light. He often speaks to us and tries to fool us into thinking we are hearing the voice of God. What better way to deceive undiscerning Christians into accepting false ideas?

I've often heard people say, "I felt God telling me to do such-and-such, and I can't understand why it turned out so badly!" But the "such-and-such" that they felt God telling them to do was a blatant violation of Scripture. God will never tell us to violate what he has already commanded in his Word. But Satan, mimicking the voice of God, will tell us, again and again, to violate God's Word.

"This is a *special* situation," Satan will say. "The rules in the Bible are *general* rules, but they don't apply to these *special* conditions." Don't believe it! The Bible's commandments and rules are unvarying principles that always hold true. I'm not talking about the dietary and sacrificial commands that God gave to Israel in the time of Moses—those were given for a specific cultural context. But God's commandments about morality, marriage, loving one another, forgiving one another, seeking God's kingdom, and so forth are universal, and they apply to us all without exception.

People often think they hear God speaking when they are really listening to the urges of the flesh or the enticements of the enemy. The reason we easily mistake Satan's voice for the voice of God is that, in this world, Satan *is* the reigning god. That's why Paul, in 2 Corinthians 4:4, calls Satan "the god of this age" (or in the King James

Version, "the god of this world"). For all who are not citizens of the kingdom of Jesus, who are not living for Jesus and subject to his authority, Satan is the god of this world.

In Exodus 7, Moses and Aaron stood before Pharaoh, threw down their staffs, and their staffs became snakes. What did Pharaoh's magicians do? They threw down their staffs—which also became snakes. But Aaron's staff swallowed up the staffs of the Egyptian magicians. God performs miracles—but Satan can mimic God's miracles with occult magic.

In Revelation 13:13, John tells us that Satan's forgery of Jesus—the Antichrist—will deceive the whole world by performing "great signs, even causing fire to come down from heaven." Satan will perform many forgeries and fraudulent miracles, pretending to exhibit the power of God himself—and many people will be fooled.

We also need to remember that Satan is a preacher. He's a *diabolical* preacher, but a preacher, nonetheless. He preaches a false gospel. He preaches a false Jesus. And all his demons are preachers too.

Demonic preaching is always in demand. There are plenty of people who do not want to hear that salvation is available to us *only* through the blood of Jesus shed on the cross. And Satan and his diabolical preachers are happy to give people the false gospel, the false preaching they want to hear.

In Acts 13, Paul and Barnabas visited the island of Cyprus, which was ruled by a Roman proconsul (governor) named Sergius Paulus. The proconsul, the account tells us, was "an intelligent man" and he sent for Paul and Barnabas "because he wanted to hear the word of God." But one of the proconsul's advisors was Elymas the sorcerer, who opposed Paul and Barnabas and tried to keep the proconsul from listening to the gospel.

Paul received insight straight from the Holy Spirit, and he told Elymas, "You are a child of the devil and an enemy of everything that is right! You are full of all kinds of deceit and trickery. Will you never stop perverting the right ways of the Lord? Now the hand of the Lord is against you. You are going to be blind for a time, not even able to see the light of the sun" (see Acts 13:6-11).

Paul could see through Elymas because his eyes were opened by the Spirit of God. He could distinguish between true spirituality and false spirits, between truth and lies. He knew that Satan is a master forger and the father of lies. If you want to have the kind of discernment Paul had, if you want to distinguish between a copy and the genuine article, then you need to ask the Spirit of God to fill you with his wisdom and insight.

5. SATAN'S STRATEGY: ELEVATE CELEBRITIES

Satan loves celebrities. That's why he's so busy elevating preachers to celebrity status. Every time I look in the Christian press and hear about a celebrity preacher who has had a moral fall, I have to say I'm not surprised.

People often look at the drunk or addicted derelict in the street and say, "That's Satan's masterpiece. The devil really got his hooks into that poor guy." Well, yes, Satan does try to destroy human souls any way he can, including through addiction. But the addict who wastes his life getting high is too easy. Alcoholics and addicts are low-hanging fruit for the devil.

Satan's real masterpiece, the person he takes pride in seducing, is the superstar celebrity, the person who is exalted by the media and the public. Satan's true work of art is the celebrity businessman, the celebrity entertainer, or the celebrity preacher who is admired by millions. Celebrities are easily tripped up by their own pride. They believe their own press clippings. They look in the mirror and say, "Yes, I can see why I have so many adoring fans!"

Once the celebrity has been ensnared by pride, Satan can use him to preach diabolical lies to millions. After all, in order to maintain all those adoring fans, a celebrity has to be politically correct. He has to express tolerance and acceptance of sexual perversion and religious apostasy. I suspect that one of the reasons so many members of the clergy support same-sex marriage and "trans rights" for minors and pornographic books in public schools is that they want to be popular. They want to be seen as "tolerant" and "inclusive."

There are many "progressive" clergy who demand that the government "defund the police," "defend LGBTQ+ rights," "create a borderless society," and "promote economic equity" (that is, impose socialism). These same "progressive Christians" deny that sin is at the root of human problems. They deny that the death of Jesus on the cross is the solution to human problems—and they reject the literal, historical reality of the resurrection.

Satan's celebrity followers are like him. They think like him, talk like him, and help him spread his lies. Satan's best work is found in the beautiful people, the celebrities, the influencers who are leading their followers down the broad road that leads to hell.

6. SATAN'S SWEET SUBVERSION: OFFER SUGAR-COATED POISON PILLS

Satan is like a drug dealer whose bestselling product is sugar-coated poison pills. Though Satan is not mentioned in the parable of the prodigal son in Luke 15, he is clearly in the background of that story. It's the story of a man who had two sons, and the younger son was enticed by Satan's poison pills—the lure of women, wine, and wild living. This young man couldn't imagine a sweeter life than taking his father's estate and spending it on endless partying and fun.

The poison pill underneath the sugar coating was the fact that both the money and the "endless" partying must eventually come to an end. After the son had squandered his wealth, there was a famine in the land. To survive, the young man was reduced to feeding pigs—a humiliating occupation for a Jewish young man.

You know how the story ends—with the boy's father happily receiving his lost son back into his arms and his home. It is a parable of God's love for us. But as we seek to understand Satan's schemes and strategies, we should recognize how Satan tempts us. Hidden within the sugary coating of Satan's tempting promises is the poison pill. For the prodigal son, a life of partying was the sugar coating—and the poison pill underneath was poverty and starvation. For Adam and Eve, the delicious forbidden fruit was the sugar coating—and the poison pill inside the forbidden fruit was death and the curse of sin.

No matter how sweet the temptation Satan offers you, expect to find poison on the inside.

7. SATAN'S SUBTERFUGE: NEVER ATTACK FROM THE FRONT

Satan is a backstabber and a sneak. He rarely attacks from the front.

If you examine the full armor of God that Paul writes of in Ephesians 6, you'll notice that the armor faces forward. The belt of truth is buckled in front, the breastplate of righteousness protects the front, the shield of faith guards the front, the helmet of salvation and the sword of the Spirit face frontward. Satan knows that—and that's why he rarely attacks from the front, where your armor is strongest. He attacks from the back.

One of the ways he attacks us from behind is by enticing us into rationalizing certain "socially acceptable sins." We would never commit the big sins, such as murder or adultery or theft. But "socially acceptable sins" are so common, even in the church, that we become used to them. We don't even think of them as *real* sins, in ourselves or in others.

Examples include impatience with other people or toward God, rudeness, angry outbursts, telling people off or lashing out at perceived slights, gossiping, holding grudges, greed, being jealous of the success or possessions of others, being lazy on the job, underpaying employees, telling "little white lies," discontentment, pride, selfishness, "cutting corners" on tax forms, worldliness, and on and on.

Satan isn't stupid. He knows better than to use a frontal attack, such as suggesting, "You ought to rob a bank," or, "You ought to cheat on your wife." But if he can get you to commit "socially acceptable sins," he can worm his way into your life without giving himself away.

This is how Satan uses Christians to undermine unity and love within a church. This is how he uses believers to stifle the gospel. He finds back doors into our lives. While we are busy making sure the front door is locked and deadbolted, Satan can come and go as he pleases through the back door.

NO ONE IS SAFE

I grew up hearing stories of an Egyptian man named Antonius, who was born in the third century AD. He is often called Anthony of the Desert or the Father of All Monks, but in the stories I heard as a boy, he was called Antonius. He was a wealthy young man who donated all his wealth to the poor and went out to the desert to devote himself to prayer and meditation. I heard stories about Antonius from my parents, from my pastor and teachers, and from the man who discipled me. I'm sure that most of the tales surrounding Antonius were legends, yet all of them had a moral lesson to teach.

In one of these stories, while Antonius was living as a desert hermit, Satan assigned many demons to torture him and tempt him. They tempted him with fatigue to keep him from praying, but he only prayed more earnestly. They tortured him with hunger, but he only committed to a stricter fast so that God would bless him. They tried to torment him with lustful thoughts, but he cried out to God to focus his mind on the grace and goodness of God. No matter what temptations the demons threw at him, Antonius emerged victorious.

Satan was supremely frustrated by the failure of his demons to break Antonius's piety, so he decided to do the job himself. He found Antonius on his knees in prayer. Satan approached Antonius very quietly and gently, so that the holy man wouldn't even know he was there. Then Satan softly whispered in Antonius's ear, "Your brother has just been made Bishop of Alexandria."

Antonius leaped to his feet, shaking his fists and shouting, "My brother! Bishop of Alexandria! This is an outrage!"

Though hunger and lust had failed, the enticement of envy succeeded in causing this holy man to sin. Again, this is a legend, not a true story. But the point this story makes speaks volumes about human nature.

Satan knows how to get under the skin of even the holiest of believers. He doesn't attack from the front, by tempting us to the big, obvious sins. He slyly seduces us into committing socially acceptable sins we are scarcely aware of. He sneaks in through the back door and ambushes us when we are unwary.

So be keenly aware of sin. Be honest with yourself about sin. Don't squint at sin or look sideways at sin—confront it squarely, deal with it honestly, confess it to God, and ask him to root that sin out of your life. As you pray, remember the words of the psalmist: "If I had cherished sin in my heart, the Lord would not have listened" (Psalm 66:18). Don't let sin neutralize your prayer life and your effectiveness for Christ.

Be aware of Satan's strategies. Arm yourself for war. And be unafraid, because the mighty Spirit of the living God goes with you into the battle.

8

WIELDING YOUR SWORD

The Holy Spirit inspired the writers of the Bible, which is why we say that the Holy Spirit is the author of the Bible. That's why Paul called the Bible "the sword of the Spirit." And that's why believers who wield that sword and live under its authority will be used mightily by God. The more yielded and surrendered we are to his Spirit, the more richly the Word of God dwells in us and speaks through us.

WIELDING YOUR SWORD

In January 2023, a newly elected California congressman was sworn into office—but unlike most of his colleagues, he didn't place his hand on a Bible. He placed his hand on a rare 1939 *Superman* comic book, borrowed from the National Archives. The Peruvian-born, openly gay congressman said that "the Man of Steel" meant a lot to him because he first learned to read and write in English by reading *Superman* comic books.[1]

I do not begrudge this man his choice of reading material, but I think it speaks volumes about the decline of faith and respect for the Bible that an American congressman can replace the Scriptures with a comic book—and there's hardly a murmur of disapproval in society, much less outrage or condemnation.

I won't go so far as to say that this congressman deliberately intended to insult the nation, the voters, or the Bible. But his actions demonstrate a lack of respect for, and understanding of, our culture's traditions and values. And it reflects a lack of reverence for God and his Word.

There is a reason why politicians have traditionally taken the oath of office on a Bible. In Europe and colonial America, oaths were generally taken on a Bible to underscore the solemnity of the commitment.

George Washington famously took his presidential oath of office on a Bible in 1789, setting a precedent of respect for God's Word that has endured for more than two centuries.

When a leader takes the oath with one hand on the Bible, he or she is visibly demonstrating a sense of accountability to a higher Authority. By this act, the leader says, "I am bound by my word to the people—and by my word to God." It is also a sign of respect for our Judeo-Christian heritage.

I am convinced that the decline of respect for the Bible in Western culture is a symptom of the spiritual war of deception that Satan is waging against the Scriptures. It's part of the devil's campaign to lead us astray. Satan hates God's Word because it reminds him that both he and his plans are doomed. We must cling to the Word as if our lives and our souls depend on it—because they do.

WAITING FOR AN OPPORTUNE TIME

Jesus is our example and forerunner. He has shown us that when we suffer Satan's attack in the invisible war, the Word of God is our indispensable sword and shield. After John the Baptist baptized Jesus in the Jordan River, the Holy Spirit led Jesus into the wilderness to be tested by Satan. The account of Satan's temptation of Jesus in the wilderness is recorded in Matthew 4, Mark 1, and Luke 4. Let's look at Luke's account of this event:

> Jesus, full of the Holy Spirit, left the Jordan and was led by the Spirit into the wilderness, where for forty days he was tempted by the devil. He ate nothing during those days, and at the end of them he was hungry.
>
> The devil said to him, "If you are the Son of God, tell this stone to become bread."

Jesus answered, "It is written: 'Man shall not live on bread alone.'"

The devil led him up to a high place and showed him in an instant all the kingdoms of the world. And he said to him, "I will give you all their authority and splendor; it has been given to me, and I can give it to anyone I want to. If you worship me, it will all be yours."

Jesus answered, "It is written: 'Worship the Lord your God and serve him only.'"

The devil led him to Jerusalem and had him stand on the highest point of the temple. "If you are the Son of God," he said, "throw yourself down from here. For it is written:

"'He will command his angels concerning you
 to guard you carefully;
they will lift you up in their hands,
 so that you will not strike your foot against a stone.'"

Jesus answered, "It is said: 'Do not put the Lord your God to the test.'"

When the devil had finished all this tempting, he left him until an opportune time (Luke 4:1-13).

Three times, Satan tried to break down Jesus's defenses and tempt him to sin. Notice that Luke's account ends with a fascinating detail not recorded by Matthew or Mark. He notes that Satan left Jesus "until an opportune time." What was the next "opportune time" Satan was looking for? Most likely, it was the crucifixion.

This narrative shows that when Satan comes to attack us and tempt us, he is very strategic and deliberate in his thinking. He plans, he strategizes, he chooses his time carefully, he waits for "an opportune time." He looks for his chance to inflict maximum damage when he ambushes us.

Looking back on the times Satan has ambushed me, I can testify that Satan truly does look for opportune times. He does not vary his strategy very much because he is an imitator, not a creator. His strategy is always the same. He always tips his hand. But because we human beings are slow to learn, we allow him to defeat us again and again by that same monotonous strategy.

SATAN TIMES HIS AMBUSH

In his second letter to the believers at Corinth, Paul urges us to live righteous, forgiving lives "in order that Satan might not outwit us. For we are not unaware of his schemes" (2 Corinthians 2:11). We need to understand Satan's schemes—his mode of operation and his method of attack—so that we can be prepared and fortified for his attacks. And much of Satan's strategy can be summed up in a single phrase: "an opportune time." Satan always times his ambush for the most destructive impact possible.

In Luke 4, Satan comes to Jesus in the wilderness to tempt him. It's important that we not miss this: "For forty days he was tempted by the devil. He ate nothing during those days, and at the end of them he was hungry." Luke says that Satan has been tempting and testing Jesus throughout those forty days of fasting.

At the end of the forty days, when Jesus is weak, starved, and physically vulnerable, Satan knows that this is the opportune moment. He will never have a better chance to break the will of Jesus. So he takes the testing and tempting of Jesus up a few more notches. He unleashes his most powerful weapons.

Remember that Peter told us—from his own personal experience—that Satan is "like a roaring lion looking for someone to devour"

(1 Peter 5:8). And there are times in our lives when we are more vulnerable to demonic attack than others. There are times when we are physically and mentally weakened, when our guard is down. That's when Satan ambushes us. That's why Peter also says in that same verse, "Be alert and of sober mind." We must be watchful at all times—and especially when we are weak and vulnerable.

What is Satan's opportune time for ambushing us? It may be a time of weakness and vulnerability, as when Satan tried to ambush Jesus at the culmination of his forty-day fast. But Satan knows that there are other opportune times in our lives—windows of opportunity he will seize on but which we might not be aware of.

ALERT AND WELL EQUIPPED

I was living in the Middle East in June 1967 when the Six-Day War took place. The Six-Day War was a brief struggle between Israel and the neighboring states of Egypt, Jordan, and Syria. Tensions had been building for years, involving border clashes, terrorist attacks, and bitter words exchanged between heads of state. Egyptian dictator Gamal Abdel Nasser mobilized troops to the Sinai Peninsula and kicked out the UN peacekeepers. Then he blockaded Israel's shipping from entering the Red Sea—a move that Israel viewed as an act of war.

Expecting a military attack from its Arab neighbors to the south and east, Israel launched a preemptive strike on June 5. Israeli planes destroyed the airfields of Egypt, Jordan, and Syria, smashing their air forces before they could get off the ground. The element of surprise was decisive. During its six-day offensive, Israel captured the Sinai, West Bank, East Jerusalem, the Golan Heights, and the Gaza Strip.

But just six years later, Israel appeared to have forgotten the lessons of the Six-Day War, especially the decisive factor of the element of surprise. On October 6, 1973, during Judaism's holiest day of Yom Kippur, Egypt and Syria launched a coordinated surprise attack, catching Israel off guard. I'm grateful I was not living in the region at the time, or I might have been swept onto the battlefield along with 200,000 invading Egyptian soldiers.

The Arab states were successful during the first three days of fighting, inflicting heavy casualties on Israel. Stunned and reeling from the ambush, Israel managed to regroup and launch a counteroffensive, encircling Egypt's Third Army while pushing deep into Syrian territory. The war ended after 19 days with a ceasefire.

The Yom Kippur War was a sobering lesson for Israel. The leaders of Israel learned that their nation is far more vulnerable than they realized.

This same lesson applies to spiritual warfare. We know that Satan uses the element of surprise. We know that he plans to ambush us—but we don't know where, when, and how the next ambush will take place.

But even though there is an element of surprise in Satan's attacks, there are things we can do to fortify and prepare ourselves. There are conditions in our lives that can leave us wide open to Satan's attacks. So we must be alert and well equipped to resist his attacks.

In chapter 4, we examined the seven pieces of the whole armor of God. Let's take another look at one key verse: "Therefore put on the full armor of God, so that when the day of evil comes, you may be able to stand your ground, and after you have done everything, to stand" (Ephesians 6:13). What is the "day of evil" that Paul refers to? It is Satan's opportune time, the moment he is waiting for when he knows you'll be vulnerable to temptation.

Satan's opportune time can take many forms in your life and mine. Let's take a closer look at some of the specific opportune times in our lives that leave us vulnerable to attack.

OPPORTUNE TIME NUMBER 1: AFTER A SPIRITUAL VICTORY

One of the most vulnerable times in our lives is immediately after a spiritual victory. After we experience a time of great blessing, great achievement, or great joy, we can easily feel spiritually invincible. And that feeling of invincibility is a warning sign—a symptom of how dangerously vulnerable we actually are.

You can probably recall spiritual "mountaintop experiences" when you were fired up to serve God, to obey God, to witness for Jesus to everyone you know. Then, within a few days, you tumbled into a valley of spiritual discouragement or disobedience. I have experienced this. I'm sure you have as well.

Satan tried to ambush Jesus in this very same way. All four Gospels tell the story of John the Baptist preaching and baptizing people in the Jordan River. When Jesus came to the river, John announced him to the people: "Look, the Lamb of God, who takes away the sin of the world!" (John 1:29). John baptized Jesus, and when Jesus came up out of the water, the Spirit of God alighted on him and a voice from heaven said, "This is my Son, whom I love; with him I am well pleased" (see Matthew 3:16-17).

This was a moment of spiritual victory in the life and ministry of Jesus. In fact, it is the most dramatic moment in human history. This is the moment when God the Father confirms Jesus's identity as God the Son, announcing the arrival of God in human flesh, appearing before human witnesses.

But this moment of victory soon passes. As Matthew's Gospel tells us, "Then Jesus was led by the Spirit into the wilderness to be tempted by the devil" (Matthew 4:1). The words of God the Father are still ringing in his ear: "This is my Son, whom I love." But in the other ear, he soon hears the sly taunt of Satan: "If you are the Son of God…"

While Jesus was coming up out of the River Jordan, while he was spiritually on top of the world, what was Satan doing? He was plotting to send Jesus crashing down. While God the Father was announcing that he was "well pleased" with his Son, Jesus, Satan was plotting the downfall of Jesus.

This is one of Satan's most opportune times. He frequently attacks immediately after we have experienced the thrill of spiritual victory. We need to be especially watchful after we have experienced the power of God, the blessing of God, and the approval of God. We need to be on our guard after we have seen God answer our prayers in a mighty way.

It doesn't surprise us that Satan would attack us when we are weakest—but we are almost never prepared to face his attacks when we are at our strongest. One reason why a time of victory is one of Satan's most opportune times is that this is when we feel the least dependent on God. We feel we are standing tall, and we have no need to spend time in prayer. We don't feel vulnerable—and that's why we're more vulnerable than ever.

Notice I said "we feel…we feel" or "we don't feel." That's the problem with relying on our feelings—our feelings are often wrong. Our feelings easily lead us astray.

There are very few Christians who can handle spiritual success well. There are very few who can handle God's blessings well. There are very few believers who know how to handle victory well. And Satan knows that. That's why Satan lurks in the dark. He is waiting for you when you are glowing with inner victory, when you are rejoicing over God's blessings. He is waiting for just the right moment to—*wham!*—hit you when you aren't looking.

Satan is waiting for that perfect moment when you start feeling proud of your spiritual success. He understands the spiritual principle that the Bible warns us about: "Pride goes before destruction, a haughty spirit before a fall" (Proverbs 16:18).

Has God opened the windows of heaven and blessed you mightily? Have you just experienced a major victory over sin? Have you just received an answer to prayer? Have you just led someone to the Lord? Have you just received a great honor? Have you experienced the fulfillment of a dream? Have you just accomplished great things for God?

If so—watch out! Satan has you in his sights. This is one of Satan's opportune times. You are on Satan's most-wanted list.

What is the solution to Satan's Opportune Time Number 1? How can you defend yourself? There is only one answer: Be watchful and alert after any spiritual victory. Cling to the Lord. Devote yourself to prayer and meditating on the Word. Take time to praise and worship the Lord. Turn Satan's opportune time into an opportunity to grow closer to God.

OPPORTUNE TIME NUMBER 2: BEFORE A SPIRITUAL VICTORY

While Satan's Opportune Time Number 1 is immediately *after* a great victory, Opportune Time Number 2 is immediately *before* a great victory.

Whenever you decide to do something great for God, whenever you are about to experience some of the greatest blessings you will ever receive, whenever you begin to see God answering your prayers—Satan will swoop in and try to steal the victory from you. He'll try to steal your blessing. He'll try to destroy your joy and derail your obedience.

We see this principle at work in the life of Jesus as well. Immediately after his temptation in the wilderness, Jesus began his public ministry. After his time in the wilderness, he began preaching and teaching throughout Palestine. He performed miracle after miracle. He was about to challenge the corrupt religious hierarchy and launch God's plan to save lost humanity. He was about to open the door of heaven to all who put their trust in him.

And Satan wanted to stop that. He wanted to divert Jesus from the greatest mission in human history. He wanted to stop the ministry of salvation in its tracks. So, after tempting and tormenting Jesus for 40 days, Luke tells us, Satan "left him until an opportune time."

But what did Jesus do at that moment? Luke writes, "Jesus returned to Galilee in the power of the Spirit, and news about him spread through the whole countryside. He was teaching in their synagogues, and everyone praised him" (see Luke 4:13-15). Jesus launched his public ministry. He set out on his mission of teaching, healing, and saving the lost. But before Jesus set off on his mission, Satan emptied his arsenal of temptation at him, hoping to keep him from reaching his goal.

It often happens that our greatest victory lies just around the corner from Satan's most vicious attack. Satan is no fool. He will try to sabotage your mission before you even begin. He will try to discourage you and prevent you from opening your hands to receive God's blessings.

When you are in Satan's line of fire, it's because he knows something you don't know. Satan isn't omniscient, and he doesn't know the future, but Satan does understand the workings of spiritual reality better than we do. He can tell when the thing you have patiently waited for and prayed for is about to be delivered. So he will tempt you to sin and surrender to defeat just when you are on the brink of victory.

Satan wants you to miss out on the victory. He wants you to miss out on answered prayer. He wants you to miss out on what God has planned for you.

OPPORTUNE TIME NUMBER 3: WHEN YOU ARE EXHAUSTED

You've almost certainly experienced this in your own life. Satan's Opportune Time Number 3 comes when you are physically, mentally, or emotionally drained. Your energy level is low. You feel listless, unmotivated, and spent. Your resistance is at low ebb. You're exhausted and vulnerable—and Satan knows it.

That's when Satan comes to you and whispers tempting suggestions in your ear. This is his opportune moment.

During the temptation in the wilderness, Jesus ate nothing for 40 days, "and at the end of them he was hungry" (Luke 4:2). The phrase "he was hungry" is a masterpiece of understatement.

Medical scientists tell us that people can live without food for a maximum of about 60 days. But long before a person dies from starvation, the body undergoes major changes. After just a few days of fasting, the lack of energy and nutrients in the body can take a toll on a person's mind and body. During the first few weeks, the body consumes glycogen in the liver and muscles for energy, leading to extreme fatigue. Internal organs begin to shut down. All of this was going on in Jesus's body—plus he was mentally exhausted from the ordeal of being tormented day and night by Satan.[2]

It was during this time of extreme hunger and vulnerability that the devil unleashed his most cruel attack. "If you are the Son of God," Satan said, "tell this stone to become bread." Jesus was literally starving to death—and Satan taunted him, dangling the prospect of bread before a starving man.

Jesus refused Satan's challenge and replied, "It is written: 'Man shall not live on bread alone.'"

It is vitally important that we understand this principle: When we are physically depleted, we are especially vulnerable to temptation and sin, and it is then that we often feel too tired to pray, too spent to focus on God. Lack of sleep, long hours of work, and mental stress can make us susceptible to temptation.

- If you are a mother with a small baby who keeps you up all night…

- If you are a businessman working long hours to build your business without getting adequate rest…

- If you provide round-the-clock care for a sick child or an aging parent…

- If you are a doctor, nurse, firefighter, police officer, soldier, or truck driver who works irregular shifts…

Watch out! This may be Satan's opportune time in your life. The physical and mental hazards of sleep deprivation are well known: impaired judgment, slow reaction times, and an increased risk of errors and accidents. But people seldom stop to consider that a lack of rest and sleep may also leave you at higher risk for temptation and satanic attack.

Fatigue can affect our thinking in unexpected ways. It can make small problems seem like the end of the world. A minor annoyance can trigger an explosion of rage from a person who is physically and mentally spent. Exhaustion can tip a normally cheerful person into a gloomy pit of depression.

A time when you feel physically, mentally, and emotionally spent is Satan's opportune moment to tempt you or discourage you. Right now, today, is a good time to start memorizing Scripture passages that you can have handy the next time Satan tries to take advantage of your depleted state. Here are some examples:

- "He gives strength to the weary and increases the power of the weak. Even youths grow tired and weary, and young men stumble and fall; but those who hope in the LORD will renew their strength. They will soar on wings like eagles; they will run and not grow weary, they will walk and not be faint" (Isaiah 40:29-31).

- "Come to me, all you who are weary and burdened, and I will give you rest. Take my yoke upon you and learn from me, for I am gentle and humble in heart, and you will find rest for your souls. For my yoke is easy and my burden is light" (Matthew 11:28-30).

- "The LORD is my shepherd, I lack nothing. He makes me lie down in green pastures, he leads me beside quiet waters, he refreshes my soul. He guides me along the right paths for his name's sake" (Psalm 23:1-3).

- "He said to me, 'My grace is sufficient for you, for my power is made perfect in weakness.' Therefore I will boast all the more gladly about my weaknesses, so that Christ's power may rest on me" (2 Corinthians 12:9).

- "I can do all this through him who gives me strength" (Philippians 4:13).

- "The LORD himself goes before you and will be with you; he will never leave you nor forsake you. Do not be afraid; do not be discouraged" (Deuteronomy 31:8).

- "God is our refuge and strength, an ever-present help in trouble" (Psalm 46:1).

- "Peace I leave with you; my peace I give you. I do not give to you as the world gives. Do not let your hearts be troubled and do not be afraid" (John 14:27).

- "When anxiety was great within me, your consolation brought me joy" (Psalm 94:19).

- "Because of the LORD's great love we are not consumed, for his compassions never fail. They are new every morning; great is your faithfulness" (Lamentations 3:22-23).

- "Do not fear, for I am with you; do not be dismayed, for I am your God. I will strengthen you and help you; I will uphold you with my righteous right hand" (Isaiah 41:10).

If you know people who are going through a trial of weariness and fatigue, remember to pray for them, asking God to give them rest and peace, and to defend them from Satan's attacks. Send them handwritten notes of encouragement, a text message, an email, a bookmark or wall art with an encouraging Bible verse—or call or visit them and pray with them. Your act of faithfulness and friendship may be their only defense against the attacks of Satan.

OPPORTUNE TIME NUMBER 4: WHEN YOU ARE WAITING

Another moment of vulnerability is Opportune Time Number 4: When You Are Waiting—specifically, when you are waiting for an answer to prayer. I will confess to you that there are few more difficult times in my life than times of waiting for God to act. I'm impatient by nature. It's hard for me to wait. I want to hurry God along.

And Satan, that master psychologist, knows that it's when we are growing frustrated and impatient that he has an opportunity. That is one of his opportune times.

It's not surprising, then, to see Satan attack Jesus in this very area of life—the area of waiting patiently. Luke writes, "The devil led him up to a high place and showed him in an instant all the kingdoms of the world. And he said to him, 'I will give you all their authority and splendor; it has been given to me, and I can give it to anyone I want to. If you worship me, it will all be yours'" (Luke 4:5-7).

What is Satan doing? He's trying to get Jesus to take a shortcut. All the kingdoms of the world ultimately belong to Jesus. Psalm 2 is a psalm of the Messiah (it is quoted as a messianic prophecy in Acts 13:33 and Hebrews 1:5). The psalmist writes:

> He said to me, "You are my son;
>   today I have become your father.
> Ask me,
>   and I will make the nations your inheritance,
>   the ends of the earth your possession" (Psalm 2:7-8).

God the Father will give all the kingdoms of the earth to Jesus the Son—but only after the cross. God already promised the ends of the earth to Jesus, but Jesus had to be patient. He had to wait and patiently endure the shame and suffering and loneliness of the cross. He had to wait for the Father's timing.

Satan controls the systems of this world, and he owns the kingdoms of the earth. So he was not making an empty offer. He truly could have given Jesus the kingdoms of the world. Satan was saying, in effect, "Why wait for God to give you tomorrow what I can give you today? Why pay the awful price of crucifixion when I can give it all to you *for free*—right *now*?" But Jesus could only accept Satan's offer by defying the will and the plan of God the Father.

Jesus could have avoided having to wait to receive those kingdoms—and he could have avoided the cross. But he resisted the temptation, rejected Satan's offer, and chose obedience.

How did Satan come into possession of the kingdoms of the earth? We find the answer to that question in the opening pages of Genesis. There we read that God made the first human beings, Adam and Eve. Genesis 1:26-28 tells us that God gave the first human beings his delegated authority to rule over the earth, to have dominion over all the plant and animal species in the world. In a symbolic sense, God gave Adam a deed to the entire planet.

God said, in effect, "Adam, you are in charge of Planet Earth. You are my steward of this world, and I am delegating my authority to you." But when Adam disobeyed God, he took that deed and signed it over to Satan. He obeyed Satan, and in so doing, he forfeited his dominion over the planet to Satan. And that is why Satan has ruled the kingdoms of the earth ever since.

But God's plan is to repossess the earth from Satan and give dominion over the planet to Jesus the Son. But Jesus can only do so after paying the price for your sin, my sin, and Adam's sin. He paid that price on the cross of Calvary.

Satan and his demonic agents know us well. They know that waiting is hard for everybody. We do not like to wait for God's timing. We would rather take a shortcut—and that is exactly what Satan will tempt us to do. That is why, again and again, God's Word encourages us to wait upon the Lord and his timing. Here are a few examples:

- "The LORD will fight for you; you need only to be still" (Exodus 14:14).

- "Wait for the LORD; be strong and take heart and wait for the LORD" (Psalm 27:14; see also Psalm 33:20-22 and 130:5-6).

- "The LORD is a God of justice. Blessed are all who wait for him!" (Isaiah 30:18).

- "Be patient, then, brothers and sisters, until the Lord's coming. See how the farmer waits for the land to yield its valuable crop, patiently waiting for the autumn and spring rains. You, too, be patient and stand firm, because the Lord's coming is near" (James 5:7-8).

Are you waiting patiently on God? Are you waiting for God's healing or blessing? Are you waiting for him to answer your prayers? Be careful and remember that this may be Satan's opportune time to attack you. Be strong, be patient, and cling to the unfailing promises of God.

OPPORTUNE TIME NUMBER 5:
WHEN YOU ARE IN THE HOUSE OF GOD

The next time of spiritual vulnerability may surprise you: Opportune Time Number 5: When You Are in the House of God.

We normally don't think of church as a place of temptation.

We assume we will be tempted out there in the world, not while we are safely ensconced in the church pew. We don't expect to be vulnerable to temptation as we sing hymns of praise and listen to the preaching of the Word of God. Surely Satan and his demons would not think we are vulnerable to attack during a worship service, would they?

But I'm going to tell you something that I have learned through painful experience and from the Word of God. When Satan tempts us in church, those temptations are far more dangerous than his attacks upon us out in the world. Why? For one thing, church is the last place you would expect to be tempted to sin. For another, the temptation that comes to you in church is usually camouflaged, so you don't even recognize it as temptation.

Sometimes, temptation can even take the form of the quoting of Scripture. When someone in church quotes God's Word but twists its meaning or applies it outside of its intended context, the result can be serious error and false doctrine.

Luke tells us that Satan led Jesus to Jerusalem, to the highest point of the temple—the house of God. Then Satan said, "If you are the Son of God, throw yourself down from here. For it is written: 'He will command his angels concerning you to guard you carefully; they will lift you up in their hands, so that you will not strike your foot against a stone'" (see Luke 4:9-11).

Satan knows the Bible. He's an expert at twisting God's Word to suit his purpose. So Satan took Jesus to the temple, the great house of worship and spiritual learning. It was the house of prayer. The Jews believed the temple was the house where God dwelled and where his glory was to be manifested. They thought a person could not get closer to God than in the temple.

You might think that Satan would keep his distance from the temple. Yet Satan took Jesus there and quoted the Bible to him there.

And he won't hesitate to treat you the same way, tempting you and misleading you in church.

Why would Satan target you while you're in church? Why is that an opportune time for him to attack? It's because that's the time and place where you open your heart to God—and when temptation is the furthest thing from your mind. It's the place where God's Word pierces you like a sharp-edged sword, dealing with your most urgent spiritual issues and needs. The Word of God is cutting into you like a surgeon's scalpel, performing open-heart surgery.

When surgeons conduct a surgical procedure, the goal of the surgeon is to restore the patient to good health. But there are risks in any surgery—and one of those risks is infection. The moment the scalpel makes the incision, the patient becomes vulnerable to microorganisms. That's why the surgical site and all the surgical instruments are carefully, meticulously sterilized.

There is a similar principle in our spiritual life. When your heart is open and pierced by the Word of God, when you are under the conviction of the Holy Spirit, Satan will do his best to infect your spiritual "incision" with temptation, doubt, and despair, all in an attempt to keep God from working in your life. At such times, you can choose one of two responses: 1) You can respond in humility, repentance, and grateful obedience, or 2) you can allow Satan to infect your heart with bitterness and rebellion. You can allow the Holy Spirit to heal you, or you can leave the church service with an infection of indifference or outright rejection.

The two-edged surgical knife of God's Word opens the heart—but once your heart is opened, you are free to choose what happens next. You can allow the Holy Spirit to do his healing work of conviction in your soul and spirit, or you can listen to the whispering of Satan: "Don't listen to the preaching. Don't listen to the Bible. You don't need to change the way you live. You don't need to repent of your sins.

You're just fine as you are. Don't get caught up in the emotions of the moment. There's plenty of time to make a decision—tomorrow or years from now. Don't rush into anything. Don't surrender to God. Maintain control of your life."

Those thoughts will come to us—and they will seem like they are our own thoughts. But they have all the hallmarks of Satan's whisperings.

HOW TO PUT YOUR ENEMY TO FLIGHT

The Holy Spirit inspired the writers of the Bible, which is why we say that the Holy Spirit is the author of the Bible. That's why Paul called the Bible "the sword of the Spirit." And that's why believers who wield that sword and live under its authority will be used mightily by God. The more yielded and surrendered we are to his Spirit, the more richly the Word of God dwells in us and speaks through us.

God does not call us to hide from the enemy. God does not call us to outsmart the enemy. God does not call us to cleverly debate the enemy. He calls us to plead the blood of Jesus and to fend off Satan's attacks with the sword of the Spirit, the Word of God. He calls us to take our stand, trusting in the Word of God and obedient to the authority of the Word of God. Do this—and you will put the enemy to flight.

The Word of God is faultless. The Word of God is complete and authoritative. The Word of God is effective and decisive. The Word of God is the source of all victory. The Word of God is the guide to truth and reality. The Word of God slices through human excuses and defenses. It pierces the conscience and brings the spiritually dead back to life. It is our dependable source of strength and wisdom in times of weariness and temptation.

As Paul reminds us, "No temptation has overtaken you except what is common to mankind. And God is faithful; he will not let you be tempted beyond what you can bear. But when you are tempted, he will also provide a way out so that you can endure it" (1 Corinthians 10:13). You are not going through anything that the saints of God haven't endured down through the centuries.

Yes, we have new technologies. We have smartphones and computers and social media. There are new technological ways of facilitating temptation and sin—but the sins of lust, hatred, anger, pride, envy, laziness, and greed are as old as humanity. The fact that we can now indulge these sins with a few mouse clicks or taps on a touchscreen does not change our fallen nature one iota.

The fact that temptation is nothing new should comfort us. It means that all of God's saints, ever since the fall of humanity, have been tempted in the same way we are today. These are different times, but both Satan's strategy and God's solution to sin remain the same.

Whose voice are you listening to? Which voice will you obey? The voice of the Holy Spirit and the Word of God? Or the voice of the enemy who wants to destroy you, your family, and your church? You must choose obedience to one—or the other. And the choice you make will echo through eternity, for good or ill. I pray you will choose wisely and righteously, in reliance on the wisdom of God's Word.

9
RECOVERY FROM FAILURE

As heirs of the everlasting kingdom, we already stand on higher ground. Wake up to this fact. We have already received everything we need to be victorious over our enemies. We have aerial superiority. We have Satan in our bombsights, and we have the spiritual firepower to send him scurrying in fear. So use that spiritual firepower.

RECOVERY FROM FAILURE

During World War II, the Luftwaffe—the air force of Hitler's Germany—flew countless missions over England, raining destruction on airfields, naval facilities, factories, and cities. Thousands of soldiers and civilians died during the Battle of Britain (July to October 1940) and the Blitz (the brutal nighttime air raids lasting from September 1940 to May 1941).

At first it seemed that Nazi Germany had aerial superiority in these battles. Hitler's plan was to bomb the English people into submission, forcing them to accept peace on Germany's terms. But the German air raids only stiffened the resolve of the English people to fight harder. Great Britain's Royal Air Force took to the clouds to knock German bombers out of the sky and prevent a planned German invasion.

By 1943, the combined air forces of Great Britain and the United States had turned the tables on Germany. America's B-17 Flying Fortress could fly higher than 30,000 feet—beyond the reach of German antiaircraft artillery and fighters. Once it became clear that the Allies had achieved aerial superiority, they were well on their way to winning the war.[1]

As one strategic analyst later concluded, "Anyone who dominates the air and space can also dictate the battlefield."[2]

AERIAL SUPERIORITY FOR SPIRITUAL BATTLES

You may wonder why I'm looking back at events that happened so long ago. It's because there's an important analogy between those aerial battles in World War II and the invisible war that rages around us today. God's strategy for winning the invisible war is to give each of us—you, me, and all believers—*aerial superiority* for our spiritual battles.

This principle comes straight from the Word of God—specifically, from the book of Ephesians, where Paul writes:

> I pray that the eyes of your heart may be enlightened in order that you may know the hope to which he has called you, the riches of his glorious inheritance in his holy people, and his incomparably great power for us who believe. That power is the same as the mighty strength he exerted when he raised Christ from the dead and seated him at his right hand in the heavenly realms, far above all rule and authority, power and dominion, and every name that is invoked, not only in the present age but also in the one to come (Ephesians 1:18-21).

I hope you read that passage with care. I want you to take special note of Paul's statement that God "raised Christ from the dead and seated him at his right hand in the heavenly realms, far above all rule and authority, power and dominion, and every name that is invoked." The next time you are troubled by the news, by stories of wars and political intrigue and nuclear saber-rattling, remember that God the Father has placed Jesus at his right hand in the heavenly realms, far above all other powers and authorities on the earth.

There are many famous names in the world today—names of presidents and dictators, celebrities and influencers, terrorists and scoundrels, billionaires and oligarchs. The power of those names is magnified many times over by the news media and social media. But it doesn't matter how powerful a name may be on this earth. Jesus is above that name—not only in this age, but in the age to come.

When God the Father raised the Son from the dead, he gave him the highest spiritual altitude possible. No one can ever approach the high position of Jesus. God placed Jesus "far above all rule and authority, power and dominion, and every name." God placed Jesus far above the angelic realm and far above Satan and his demons.

And God placed Jesus above all your circumstances and above all the events of history. This is a fulfillment of the prophecy of the psalmist, who wrote, "The LORD says to my lord: 'Sit at my right hand until I make your enemies a footstool for your feet'" (Psalm 110:1).

IN THE HEAVENLY REALMS WITH JESUS

At this point, you might be thinking, *Well, that's good news for Jesus— but how does that help me? Jesus is above all authority and power, and he's above every name—but I'm not. I'm still here on Earth, dealing with spiritual battles and pressures and worries. How does any of this help me?*

If that's what you're thinking, I have good news. Writing under the inspiration of the Holy Spirit, Paul read your mind and anticipated your question. In the second chapter of Ephesians, he writes:

> Because of his great love for us, God, who is rich in mercy, made us alive with Christ even when we were dead in transgressions—it is by grace you have been saved. And God raised us up with Christ and seated us with him in the heavenly realms in Christ Jesus (Ephesians 2:4-6).

Take careful note of these phrases: God "made us alive with Christ" and "raised us up with Christ." God the Father not only raised the

Son, but he also raised us as well. As a result, you and I are seated with Jesus in the heavenly realms.

This is a profound truth. We easily forget that God raised us up with Jesus and placed us in the heavenly realm with Jesus. Whether you are reading this book in your easy chair or in a hospital bed or at your office desk or in a prison cell or listening to it as an audiobook in your car, if you are a born-again follower of Jesus, *you're not sitting where you think you are*. God has raised you up with Jesus and has seated you with Jesus in the heavenly realms. Right now, at this very moment, you are sitting in the heavenly realms with Jesus.

This is *how* God sees you, and this is *where* God sees you. This is not an illusion. This is not a metaphor. This is spiritual reality. It's an invisible reality, but it is no less real just because your eyes are not designed to perceive it. Just as the invisible war is real, this invisible reality—the fact that we are seated with Jesus in the heavenly realms—is utterly real. You are sitting in the heavenly places *right now*.

We don't have to do anything to get there. We are *already* there.

OUR HIGH-ALTITUDE ADVANTAGE

We are at war. It is a real war, an intense struggle. We can't see the enemy, but he's real and he's extremely dangerous. He hates our Commander, he hates us, he hates our families, and he's bent on our complete destruction.

Our enemy is determined to destroy our children's faith and moral values. Our enemy is determined to shake the foundation of our society and the church. Our enemy is determined to destroy the Christian church.

But our enemy will fail.

As heirs of the everlasting kingdom, we already stand on higher ground. Wake up to this fact. We have already received everything we need to be victorious over our enemies. We have aerial superiority.

We have Satan in our bombsights, and we have the spiritual firepower to send him scurrying in fear. So use that spiritual firepower.

We are the children of the King. Live like it!

We are the redeemed of the Lord. Act like it!

We are the army of the living God. Believe it and be confident!

The forces that control the skies always have the advantage. You want to be on the heights, looking down at your enemy. And that's exactly the advantage God has given you in the invisible war. He gave you that advantage when he saved you and set you in the heavenly realms with Jesus.

We are ambushed and trapped when we forget our position and abandon the heights. Satan can't win the invisible war, but he can win the skirmish by tricking us into leaving our high ground. We surrender our advantage to the enemy when we descend into the valley where he lurks—and he will ruthlessly exploit that mistake.

Believe me, I have made that mistake. I'm not telling you anything I haven't first told myself. If Satan can trick you into descending to his level and plunging into disobedience, doubt, and unbelief, he will exploit your vulnerability without mercy. If he can make you forget *who* you are and *whose* you are and *where* you are in the heavenly realms, he will make you feel defeated. If he can make you forget for even a few moments, he can neutralize your effectiveness for God.

THE THREE BROAD CATEGORIES OF TEMPTATION

There are three major areas of life, three major forms of temptation, in which your enemy will try to topple you from the high-altitude realm that is God's will for your life. These three forms of temptation are Satan's windows of opportunity to defeat you. Every moral and spiritual failure you have ever experienced falls under one of these three broad categories of temptation—and these categories come straight from God's Word.

The apostle John heard Jesus describe his own experience of being tempted by Satan in the wilderness. Reflecting on the three wilderness temptations of Jesus, John writes: "For everything in the world—the lust of the flesh, the lust of the eyes, and the pride of life—comes not from the Father but from the world" (1 John 2:16). These three categories of temptation run parallel to the three temptations of Jesus in the wilderness.

The lust of the flesh, the lust of the eyes, and the pride of life are the three surface-to-air missiles Satan will use against you to knock you out of the heavenly realms and send you crashing to the ground. These three categories of temptation encompass every temptation we ever experience.

Satan took aim at Jesus in each of these three areas—and Jesus fended off and defeated Satan every time. The Bible tells us, "We do not have a high priest who is unable to empathize with our weaknesses, but we have one who has been tempted in every way, just as we are—yet he did not sin" (Hebrews 4:15). And because of his sinlessness, Jesus can take upon his own sinless body the sins of all believers who confess their own sin.

We took a closer look at Satan's temptation of Jesus in the wilderness in chapter 8. Let's take another look at this same incident, but from a somewhat different perspective. Jesus has been fasting for 40 days in the wilderness. The wilderness is enemy territory. I like to think of it as Satan's Las Vegas. I can easily imagine Satan gathering his demons there to have workshops and training seminars on how to tempt believers and trap them into sin and discouragement. So when Jesus went out into the wilderness, he was in enemy territory. I believe he deliberately went there to have a showdown with Satan.

I don't recommend that you attempt to square off with the devil. I wouldn't do it. At the most, I might venture into enemy territory to rescue someone else from the clutches of Satan. Though we are, in general, to be imitators of Christ, we are not strong enough to do everything Jesus could do, such as going face-to-face with Satan.

In chapter 8, we looked at Luke's account of the Lord's temptation in the wilderness. In this chapter, let's look at Matthew's account, which brings out some interesting facets of the same event:

> Jesus was led by the Spirit into the wilderness to be tempted by the devil. After fasting forty days and forty nights, he was hungry. The tempter came to him and said, "If you are the Son of God, tell these stones to become bread."
>
> Jesus answered, "It is written: 'Man shall not live on bread alone, but on every word that comes from the mouth of God.'"
>
> Then the devil took him to the holy city and had him stand on the highest point of the temple. "If you are the Son of God," he said, "throw yourself down. For it is written:
>
> > "'He will command his angels concerning you,
> >   and they will lift you up in their hands,
> >   so that you will not strike your foot against a stone.'"
>
> Jesus answered him, "It is also written: 'Do not put the Lord your God to the test.'"
>
> Again, the devil took him to a very high mountain and showed him all the kingdoms of the world and their splendor. "All this I will give you," he said, "if you will bow down and worship me."
>
> Jesus said to him, "Away from me, Satan! For it is written: 'Worship the Lord your God, and serve him only.'"
>
> Then the devil left him, and angels came and attended him (Matthew 4:1-11).

This passage tells us that the Holy Spirit led Jesus into the wilderness to be tempted by Satan. This was not an accidental encounter. The Holy Spirit planned this confrontation. God was setting the stage for a conflict that would lead directly to Satan's defeat on the cross of Calvary.

LITERALLY STARVING TO DEATH

Next, Matthew tells us that after Jesus had fasted for 40 days and 40 nights, he was hungry. He was undoubtedly weak from hunger and suffering many ill effects from a month and ten days of malnutrition. It was then that Satan came to Jesus and said, "If you are the Son of God, tell these stones to become bread."

People often say when it's getting close to dinnertime, "I'm starving!" But Jesus was literally starving to death. The prospect of having bread to eat was more than just tempting—it was a matter of life and death. Hunger will drive a starving man to do things he would never do with a full stomach.

In John 4, there's an incident after Jesus's conversation with the Samaritan woman at Jacob's well. The disciples approached Jesus and said, "Rabbi, eat something." Jesus replied, "I have food to eat that you know nothing about." His baffled disciples said to each other, "Could someone have brought him food?"

Jesus said, "My food is to do the will of him who sent me and to finish his work" (see John 4:31-34). He was telling them, in other words, "My obedience to the Father sustains me in ways you don't understand. Obedience to the Father is my food as the divine Son of God."

Being fully God, Jesus was sustained by his obedience to God's will. Yet, being fully human, he shared our needs, our pain, and our suffering—including the pangs of hunger. When Satan inflicted these torments on Jesus at the end of his fast, the temptation was real, and it was intense. The exact nature of the temptation is also amazingly subtle—so subtle that if you are not alert to it, you might miss it.

In the original Greek, the words that are translated "*If* you are the Son of God" could also be translated "*Since* you are the Son of God." In fact, I believe that the more accurate translation should be, "*Since* you are the Son of God, tell these stones to become bread." This would mean that Satan was not testing Jesus to find out whether or not he was the Son of God—he knew exactly who Jesus was.

I don't believe Satan was questioning the divinity of Jesus. I don't believe Satan was questioning whether Jesus the Son was with God the Father before the creation of the world. In fact, Satan seems to be intimating that he knows who Jesus is. He remembers being in the presence of God the Son before being cast out of heaven.

During this encounter in the wilderness, Satan recognizes Jesus for who he is—and he says, "Since you are the Son of God, tell these stones to become bread." In effect, he's saying, "You and I both know that you have the power to turn these stones into bread. What's stopping you?"

"HARMLESS" TEMPTATION—OR THE LUST OF THE FLESH?

Satan seems to make a perfectly reasonable suggestion. Jesus is hungry. He has the power to make bread. His Father has given him the authority to perform miracles. There's no law that says he shouldn't. Why shouldn't he make bread? What would be the harm?

From a human perspective, this doesn't even qualify as a temptation. Satan is simply offering him a commonsense solution to his hunger. This is how our entire culture thinks. If it meets your wants or needs, and it doesn't hurt anybody, just do it. Who will be hurt if you satisfy your lusts outside of marriage? Just do it. Who will be hurt if you fudge on your taxes (as long as you don't get caught)? Just do it. Who will be hurt if you shoplift? A multibillion-dollar corporation? Oh, come on. Just do it! Everybody does it.

There was no reason Jesus shouldn't turn a stone into bread. Morally, it wouldn't be any different than turning water into wine at the wedding in Cana. So what was the problem? Why did Jesus refuse to do it?

The problem was timing. The problem was obedience. Jesus was determined not to break his fast one millisecond before the timing that God the Father had decreed.

Jesus is not saying that bread and nutrition and hunger are unimportant. He's not saying, "I don't need bread. I can get along just fine without eating." No, he's saying, "My obedience to the Father, my commitment to the Father's timing, is far more important than my hunger." That is why Jesus responds, "It is written: 'Man shall not live on bread alone, but on every word that comes from the mouth of God'" (Matthew 4:4).

The secret of Jesus's victory is the secret of your victory and mine. When Satan tries to lure you down from your high ground by appealing to your appetites, rely on God's Word. And in order to rely on the Word, you have to *know* the Word. You have to be able to say, "It is written…" to effectively wield your sword.

Satan's attempt to lure Jesus into satisfying his hunger the wrong way at the wrong time is an example of what the apostle John calls "the lust of the flesh." The lust of the flesh refers to our innate human cravings for physical satisfaction or gratification in ways that are opposed to God's will. Satan tried to use the physical hunger of Jesus to lure him into using his divine power for self-gratification. Satan tried to get Jesus to prioritize his fleshly needs over his mission and his obedience to God.

THE LUST OF THE EYES

Jesus used the Word of God to deflect Satan's first blow—but Satan wasn't finished. His attack continued. In the second temptation, Satan moves from what John calls "the lust of the flesh" to "the lust of the eyes." Satan knows that if he can get you to visualize it and see it in your mind's eye, or if he can actually place a tantalizing temptation right before your eyes—you are halfway to giving in.

Satan tries to tempt Jesus with the lust of the eyes by appealing to his ego. We all have an ego, a God-given sense of self-esteem. An ego is not a bad thing, per se. God wants us to have confidence and a sense that he loves us and wants to use us for his glory. God doesn't want us to feel worthless, useless, or contemptible.

But our egos can become unhealthy when they become inflated, when we become convinced that we are more important than other people. As Paul reminds us, "Do not think of yourself more highly than you ought, but rather think of yourself with sober judgment" (Romans 12:3). Our goal should be to *sanctify* the ego and keep our self-image under control through Christlike humility and the power of the Holy Spirit.

How does Satan tempt Jesus in the area of the lust of the eyes? He takes Jesus to the highest pinnacle in the city, and he says, in effect, "Jump! Since you are the Son of God, throw yourself down."

Understand, Satan is not suggesting that Jesus should commit suicide. He is appealing to Jesus's ego and trying to stir up the lust of the eyes in Jesus. He says, "Throw yourself down. For it is written: 'He will command his angels concerning you, and they will lift you up in their hands, so that you will not strike your foot against a stone.'"

Satan tries to put an image in Jesus's mind—the spectacular image of angels visibly catching Jesus in midair in front of crowds of eyewitnesses. Satan thinks he can tempt Jesus to seek recognition and approval in the eyes of the onlookers. He thinks he can lure Jesus into prioritizing the approval of human beings over God's timing and God's plan—and he suggests that the visual spectacle of an angelic rescue would be the perfect way to "wow" the crowds.

Satan is saying, in effect, "I couldn't tempt you into satisfying your appetite, so I will appeal to your imagination. I'll attack you in the area of the lust of the eyes. Visualize what a spectacle that would be! You believe the Word of God, don't you? Well, prove it. Prove you really do trust the promises of the Bible. Take a leap of faith."

Remember, Jesus has not even begun his public ministry yet. The testing in the wilderness came before anyone had ever heard of Jesus, before he began teaching, preaching, and healing people. So Satan urged Jesus to start his ministry with a spectacular visual stunt.

Jesus knew that the Father would have saved him if he had jumped. A thousand angelic bodyguards could have materialized and caught him in midair—a gimmick that would have made Jesus an overnight sensation.

Satan knows the Bible backward and forward. He knows the Bible so well that he trembles at its prophecy of his coming doom (if only you and I would tremble at the Word of God!). Because Satan knows the Bible so well, he is able to cleverly twist it and use it for his purposes. Be wary of those who claim to have invented a new way to interpret the Bible.

The advertising industry is based on appealing to the lust of the eyes. They show you a juicy hamburger with sizzling bacon and melting cheese—and you want it! They show you an athlete lacing up a pair of $200 sneakers—and your kids want them! They show you a middle-aged couple dancing and golfing and running on the beach—and you want the same prescription medicine they're taking!

Advertisers know how to appeal to the lust of the eyes—and so does Satan. In fact, that's how Satan deceived Eve. He directed her attention to the one forbidden tree in the garden—and she just had to have that fruit. Genesis 3:6 tells us, "The woman saw that the fruit of the tree was good for food and pleasing to the eye." It was the lust of the eyes that ensnared her.

In the book of Joshua, we read of the conquest of Jericho. Joshua had ordered all the gold and silver artifacts of Jericho to be sent to the Lord's treasury. But a man named Achan pilfered some precious items and hid them in his tent. And because of Achan's sin, the army of Israel lost its next battle at the city of Ai. When Joshua confronted Achan, the man confessed, "When I saw in the plunder a beautiful robe from Babylonia, two hundred shekels of silver and a bar of gold weighing fifty shekels, I coveted them and took them" (Joshua 7:21).

Remember those words: "When I saw…" The moment Achan yielded to the lust of the eyes, he doomed himself and caused the defeat of his nation. As Solomon wrote, "The eye never has enough of seeing" (Ecclesiastes 1:8), and "Death and Destruction are never satisfied, and neither are human eyes" (Proverbs 27:20).

When Satan tried to tempt Jesus with the lust of the eyes, Jesus replied with the sword of the Spirit, the Word of God. Quoting Deuteronomy 6:16, Jesus told Satan, "It is also written: 'Do not put the Lord your God to the test'" (Matthew 4:7).

Jesus set an example for you and me. When we are tempted by the lust of the eyes, we must always respond with the sword of the Spirit. God's Word not only defends us from attack, but it is our offensive weapon against our mortal enemy.

THE PRIDE OF LIFE

When Satan cannot trap Jesus through Plan A, the lust of the flesh, or Plan B, the lust of the eyes, he switches to Plan C, the pride of life. After striking out twice, Satan changes his tactics. Twice he has tried to appeal to *lust*. Now he appeals to *pride*.

We know what the word *pride* means—but what is "the pride of life"? The pride of life can be summed up in these words: "You can have it all now." That is what Satan is saying to Jesus: "You can have it all now. You can have all the kingdoms of the world—right now.

It doesn't matter how you get them. All that matters is that you get what you want."

Our world reverberates with advertising slogans and cultural catchphrases that appeal to the pride of life: "Because You're Worth It." "Live Your Best Life." "Just Do It." "The Best or Nothing." "Experience Amazing." "There Is No Substitute." "The Art of Being Unique." "Be Extraordinary." "Elegance Is an Attitude." "If It Feels Good, Do It." "Life Is Short—Play Hard!" "My Body, My Choice." "Be Bold, Be Proud, Be Gay."

As we saw in chapter 8, when Adam disobeyed God, he signed the deed to planet Earth over to Satan—and Satan has ruled the kingdoms of the earth ever since. That's why the Bible calls Satan "the god of this world" (see 2 Corinthians 4:4 KJV). Satan rules the world, and his demons have garrison cities around the globe to maintain their rule.

But the whole time that Satan is tempting Jesus in the wilderness, he knows that Jesus has come to challenge his ownership of planet Earth. So what does Satan do? He says to Jesus, in effect, "Let's make a deal."

Satan's demons operate much like the CIA—only their agency would be called the DIA, the Demonic Intelligence Agency. The demons examined the pages of the Old Testament, especially the messianic prophecies. They realized that there were prophecies in the Bible of a coming Messiah who would destroy the power of Satan and death. So Satan comes to Jesus in the wilderness, and he offers Jesus a deal—a friendly bargain.

In essence, Satan is saying to Jesus, "You and I both know why you're here. We both know you've come here to take the deed to planet Earth away from me. But let's settle this amicably. I'll turn everything over to you. I'll return the world to you. All the kingdoms of the world can be yours *right now* if you bow down and worship me."

Something about Satan's offer seems strangely modern to me. It has the allure of the shortcut, the enticement of instant gratification, the appeal of the elimination of pain, suffering, and effort. Just bow down, and it's all yours, instantly. Satan is offering Jesus an easy victory on the most favorable terms.

The average person today would look at the deal Satan laid out and say, "Go for it! You have nothing to lose and everything to gain. So you bow down and say some nice things about Satan. Look at all you're getting! It's a win-win! What's wrong with that?"

But this temptation is not a business deal. It's a tactic in spiritual warfare.

I have an attorney friend who has told me I need to read the fine print before signing any contract. I say, "But it's thirty pages long." He says, "The longer the contract, the more you need to read every word. There could be a poison pill hidden in all those pages." I'm very thankful for lawyers who are careful to read every word on every page.

There was a poison pill in the deal that Satan offered to Jesus. When Satan said, "All this I will give you if you will bow down and worship me," he didn't mean that Jesus should merely bow down and say some nice things about Satan. The original Greek word for "worship" is *proskyneō*. It is derived from a word used to describe a dog licking his master's hand. It means abject submission, falling on one's face in reverence, supplication, adoration, and submission. This was the hidden clause, the poison pill, in Satan's offer.

Jesus would have gotten everything he came to Earth for by taking a shortcut. He could have avoided the torment of Gethsemane. He could have escaped the cross. All he had to do was submit his will to Satan's will.

If Jesus had accepted the deal Satan offered, we might still have churches today. The churches would have no crosses on them. But there might still be preaching and the singing of hymns. But the sign in front of the church would read "Satan and Company." The sermons and the hymns would all celebrate Satan. It would not be the holy and victorious church of Jesus Christ.

MAINTAIN YOUR ALTITUDE

What is the practical importance of this account in our lives today?

In this invisible war, Jesus is not only our Commander but our Example. He has gone before us into the wilderness of temptation to show us how to overcome Satan's assaults. He has shown us how Satan's strategies work—and he exemplifies the key to fending off Satan's attacks. I hope you are sufficiently forewarned. I hope you are now fully armed and armored for battle.

You have seen that Satan will seem to offer you a generous bargain—but there's always a catch. There's always fine print. There's always a poison pill.

Whenever you find yourself tempted, ask yourself: How is Satan trying to trap me? In which of these areas is he attacking me—the lust of the flesh, the lust of the eyes, or the pride of life? Is he urging me to satisfy the lust of the flesh—my craving for food, alcohol, drugs, or sexual gratification? Or is he urging me to satisfy the lust of the eyes—my craving for selfishness and materialism, my desire to be noticed, admired, and envied? Or is he urging me to yield to the pride of life—my craving for doing *my* will, *my* way, instead of obeying the will of God?

Always ask these questions when you are tempted. Every temptation comes under one of those three areas. Understanding Satan's strategies is crucial to fending off his attacks with the sword of the Spirit, God's Word.

Satan's goal is to drive a wedge between you and God the Father. He knows that your fellowship with God is the source of your strength. He knows that if he can weaken that relationship, if he can successfully tempt you into sin, if he can paralyze you and fill you with doubt and discouragement, then he can rob you of your aerial superiority. He can topple you from your high altitude.

Always remember that God has raised us up with Jesus. We are seated with Jesus in the heavenly realms. This is not a metaphor. This is spiritual reality—and Satan wants to make you forget your spiritual altitude.

So I appeal to you to maintain your altitude. Keep your spiritual guard up. Remain on a war footing. Don't let Satan entice you or tempt you into abandoning your post in the heavenly realm. Satan's days are numbered. He will soon be vanquished, and Jesus will soon be glorified.

And that day may come sooner than you think.

10
DON'T FORGET TO BREATHE

Prayer is not just another plate of spiritual armor. It's more like the air a spiritual warrior breathes. It is not just our protection—it is life itself in spiritual warfare.

DON'T FORGET TO BREATHE

John Knox was a Scottish preacher, a leader in the Reformation movement, and the founder of the Church of Scotland. He was often at odds with Scotland's Catholic monarch, Mary, Queen of Scots, and sometimes criticized her in his sermons. Mary became so angry with Knox that she had him arrested for treason, but the court found him not guilty and released him. She once said of John Knox, "I fear his prayers more than I do the armies of my enemies."

I suspect that Satan probably felt the same way.

When Knox reached his late fifties, he became increasingly weak and chronically ill. Finally, in November 1572, Knox could no longer rise up from his bed. He knew he was dying. With his wife, children, and a few friends gathered around him, he said to his wife, "Read me that Scripture where I first cast my anchor."

The passage John Knox asked for was the high priestly prayer in John 17, which Jesus prayed shortly before going to the cross. It's a good passage of Scripture to hear in the final moments of life, and it begins, "After Jesus said this, he looked toward heaven and prayed: 'Father, the hour has come. Glorify your Son, that your Son may glorify you.'"

As Knox listened to the prayer of Jesus, he relaxed and seemed to no longer notice his pain and weakness. As his wife finished reading the passage, Knox began to pray. He interceded for loved ones and friends. He prayed for a few souls he knew who had steadfastly rejected the gospel. He prayed for the protection of believers who were suffering persecution.

As John Knox prayed, his voice grew fainter. His lips moved more slowly—then stopped. His spirit was no longer in his body. John Knox was in eternity with Jesus.[1]

He was a soldier in the invisible war—right up to the moment of his death.

Prayer is an indispensable resource in our spiritual battles. Did you notice, as we were studying the full armor of God in Ephesians 6, that Paul did *not* list prayer as a piece of that armor? Though prayer is closely related to the full armor of God, and Paul writes about prayer immediately after he writes about the armor, prayer is *not* one of the pieces of that armor.

Prayer is not just another plate of spiritual armor. It's more like the air a spiritual warrior breathes. It is not just our protection—it is *life itself* in spiritual warfare.

That is why, immediately after laying out the full armor of God in Ephesians 6, Paul writes:

> Pray in the Spirit on all occasions with all kinds of prayers and requests. With this in mind, be alert and always keep on praying for all the Lord's people. Pray also for me, that whenever I speak, words may be given me so that I will fearlessly make known the mystery of the gospel, for which I am an ambassador in chains. Pray that I may declare it fearlessly, as I should (Ephesians 6:18-20).

This is Paul's urgent appeal for spiritual alertness and for Christians to wage spiritual warfare through the power of prayer.

I have met very few believers who are satisfied with their prayer life. Whenever the subject of prayer is brought up in a Christian gathering, many people inevitably feel guilty. My prayer for you as I write these words is that, at whatever stage you're in, by the time you close this book, your prayer life will be revolutionized.

THE VITAL IMPORTANCE OF "ALL-PRAYER"

Christian parents should encourage their children to read John Bunyan's classic allegorical novel *The Pilgrim's Progress*. It has been translated into more than 200 languages, and it has remained continuously in print since its first publication in 1678. Bunyan began writing the book in the Bedfordshire County prison, where he was being punished for holding church services outside of the authority of the Church of England. I first read the book when I was 12, and it impacted me deeply.

The lead character of the novel is a man named Christian. He's an everyman character who journeys from the City of Destruction to the Celestial City (heaven). During the journey, he must persevere through the Slough of Despond (a swamp of despair and doubt), pass through the Wicket Gate (the narrow gate of salvation), face the Cross (where his burden of sin is lifted), and ascend Hill Difficulty. Finally, he arrives at House Beautiful, a welcoming refuge for weary pilgrims.

Christian's hosts at House Beautiful (which represents the church) are the sisters Discretion, Piety, Prudence, and Charity. They serve as counselors and guides to Christian, giving him spiritual food and advice for the challenges ahead. The sisters take Christian to the armory, which is stocked with equipment for spiritual warfare—enough armor and weaponry, Bunyan writes, to equip "as many men for the service of their Lord as there be stars in the heaven."

The sisters show Christian many weapons from the Bible—the

rod of Moses, the trumpets of Gideon, the ox-goad of Shamgar, the sling and stone that David hurled at Goliath, and the sword which the Lord will one day use to destroy the Antichrist. And, in a passage based on Ephesians 6:10-18, the sisters show Christian the weapons he will need for his future battles—all manner of weapons "which their Lord had provided for pilgrims, as sword, shield, helmet, breastplate, All-Prayer, and shoes that would not wear out."[2]

What is "All-Prayer"? It is the weapon of prayer which Christian must wield in order to do battle with his enemies, Apollyon and the fiends of hell. When all else fails, it is All-Prayer that enables him to achieve the victory in the Valley of the Shadow of Death.

Bunyan was a brilliant student of the Scriptures. He had a deep understanding of Ephesians 6 and the full armor of God. He understood the special role of prayer in our invisible war against the rulers, authorities, and powers of this dark world and against the spiritual forces of evil in the heavenly realms. The name "All-Prayer" comes from Ephesian 6:18: "Pray in the Spirit on *all* occasions with *all* kinds of prayers and requests. With this in mind, be alert and *always* keep on praying for *all* the Lord's people."

Look again at the words I italicized in that verse and notice how emphatic Paul is about prayer: "all…all…always…all." John Bunyan borrows Paul's emphasis on prayer, and he envisions prayer as our most powerful and effective weapon for spiritual warfare.

A SOLDIER WHO CAN'T BREATHE

Prayer is the air we breathe as soldiers in the invisible war. Imagine you're a soldier on the battlefield. You're well equipped. Your helmet is in place, you have your body armor covering all your vital organs and limbs, you have your feet properly shod.

But something is wrong. You are surrounded by clouds of dense smoke. You can't breathe! And if you can't breathe, you're defenseless.

All the body armor in the world can't help you if you can't get oxygen into your lungs and bloodstream.

Prayer is breathing. It's breathing out and breathing in. When we breathe out, we lay our requests and concerns before God. When we breathe in, we listen to the voice of God in prayer and receive the power and wisdom of the Holy Spirit.

Jesus taught his disciples that they should "always pray and not give up" (see Luke 18:1). Our Lord knows that when the battle becomes intense, we need to fill our lungs with the fresh air of prayer. The soldier who doesn't pray is in danger of becoming weak and discouraged.

When you are impressively arrayed in the armor of God, you might be tempted to think you have it all. You might think you are a super-Christian, ready for battle. Spiritual arrogance and smugness can fool us into thinking we have everything we need. We have the belt of truth cinched up, the breastplate of righteousness in place, our gospel shoes on our feet, the shield of faith in the ready position, and the helmet of salvation and the sword of the Spirit. Check, check, and check!

But it's not until we are out on the battlefield that we realize we can't breathe. We forgot to pray! And by then, it's too late. We should have made a habit of spiritual breathing long before the battle started.

SATAN'S SPECIAL TALENT

Satan has a special talent for taking God's blessings and twisting them into curses. He has a special ability to take the good things God has given us and to use them against us. He will even try to get us to feel so secure and complacent in our Ephesians 6 armor that we forget to depend on God moment by moment.

That's why prayer is so important. Prayer keeps us humble. Prayer reminds us that we can do nothing in our own strength, yet we can do all things in God's strength. Prayer keeps us in an attitude of utter dependence on God.

In some ways, the church is like a football team. We can have great talent and skills. We can have the best training and the toughest workouts. We can have the most brilliant playbook. We can have the best equipment. But if we are not in constant communication with our Head Coach, we will fail. He is the Master Strategist. He calls the winning plays. Our job is to execute those plays in complete dependence on our Coach.

Paul's letter to the Ephesians begins by lifting us up to the portals of heaven, and it concludes by pulling us down to our knees in prayer. Paul wants us to know that we have received many blessings and resources to aid us in our battle against Satan and his invisible agents. He wants us to know that God has raised us up with Jesus and has seated us with Jesus in the heavenly realms. He wants us to know that God has given us armor and weaponry with which to fight our invisible battles.

But at the same time, the Holy Spirit, speaking through the apostle Paul, wants us to be fully aware that all of these blessings and resources do not mean that we can win this war without being humbly dependent on God. We cannot even *take a breath* without being humbly dependent on God.

There's nothing magical about the full armor of God. You can have the belt of truth, the breastplate of righteousness, the gospel shoes, the shield of faith, the helmet of salvation, and the sword of the Spirit—but if you fail to live in prayerful dependence on God, you'll be as helpless as a newborn baby.

A line in James Russell Lowell's poem "Vision of Sir Launfal" expresses a profound truth: "For the gift without the giver is bare."[3] The full armor of God is an amazing array of powerful gifts to aid us in our struggle. But without the Giver of those gifts, we will fight in vain.

I've met a lot of Christians who had a great regard for biblical truth, who lived righteous lives, who could explain the gospel with clarity, who had a great faith in Jesus, who were saved, and who had a good grasp of biblical teachings—yet you could instantly sense that they had dour, dried up, hardened spirits. Why? I believe it's because they had the gift but not the Giver. They had put on the full armor of God, but they had stopped breathing. They had neglected prayer. They had lost contact with God, the Giver of the armor.

PERSEVERING IN PRAYER

Let's return to Ephesian 6:18, noting once again Paul's emphasis on the word *all*: "Pray in the Spirit on *all* occasions with *all* kinds of prayers and requests. With this in mind, be alert and *always* keep on praying for *all* the Lord's people."

My late friend John R.W. Stott, in a commentary on this verse, wrote, "Most Christians pray sometimes, with some prayers and some degree of perseverance, for some of God's people. But to replace 'some' by 'all' in each of these expressions would be to introduce us to a new dimension of prayer."[4] In other words, we need the weapon that John Bunyan calls "All-Prayer."

Let's return for a moment to *The Pilgrim's Progress*. Christian leaves House Beautiful and continues on his journey. He arrives at the Valley of the Shadow of Death, a perilous and terrifying place that symbolizes spiritual trials and terrors. The path through the valley is narrow and fraught with danger. A ditch lies on one side of the path, a quagmire on the other. The darkness of the valley is so deep that Christian can hardly see where to step.

As he reaches the middle of the valley, Christian realizes he has arrived at the mouth of hell, from which flames, smoke, sparks, and hideous sounds arise. Bunyan writes that the terror of that place was so intense that Christian is "forced to put up his sword, and betake himself to another weapon called All-Prayer."

Christian's armor alone is not enough. He needs the power of

All-Prayer. So Christian cries out, "O Lord, I beseech thee, deliver my soul!" But one prayer is not enough—he has to persevere in prayer.

He presses on while flames burst around him, evil voices call out to him, and he fears he will be torn in pieces by fiends from the darkness. He trudges on for several miles, praying as he goes—and at times he considers turning around and going back. When the fiends start to close in on him, he shouts in terror—and in fervent, desperate prayer—"I will walk in the strength of the Lord God!"[5] Only then do Christian's tormentors flee from him.

We need to put on the full armor of God. But the armor of God will not help us without a constant reliance on prayer. Clad in God's armor, let us go forth to battle, praying in the Spirit on *all* occasions, laying out *all* of our prayers and requests for *all* of God's people, remaining alert at *all* times and *always* persevering in prayer.

ALERT IN PRAYER

We should take special note of Paul's final admonition in Ephesians 6:18: "With this in mind, be alert and always keep on praying for all the Lord's people."

The Word of God calls us to pray at all times, persistently and continually, in every way imaginable. We are to pray publicly and privately. We are to pray in loud cries and soft whispers. We are to pray deliberately from a prayer journal, and we are to pray spontaneously, in a moment of sudden need. We are to pray while standing, sitting, kneeling, or lying down. We are to pray at home, at church, in the car, and while exercising. We are to pray with our hands raised or folded. We are to pray with our eyes closed or open. We are to pray with our head bowed or our face lifted to the heavens.

Wherever you are, pray. Whatever you are doing, pray. Whether you are happy or depressed, pray. Whether you are enjoying God's blessings or are in dire distress, pray.

Our Muslim friends pray five times a day. If they forget and miss a prayer time, they have a short period of time to make it up. If they fail to pray in time, then that prayer time was simply spoiled, like a piece of fruit that goes bad.

In the Old Testament, the Israelites prayed three times daily—morning, noon, and evening. But in the New Testament, we are encouraged, again and again, to pray continually, faithfully, without ceasing. Here are some examples:

- "Jesus told his disciples a parable to show them that they should always pray and not give up" (Luke 18:1).
- "Be joyful in hope, patient in affliction, faithful in prayer" (Romans 12:12).
- "Pray continually" (1 Thessalonians 5:17).
- "By prayer and petition, with thanksgiving, present your requests to God" (Philippians 4:6).
- "The prayer of a righteous person is powerful and effective" (James 5:16).
- "This is the confidence we have in approaching God: that if we ask anything according to his will, he hears us" (1 John 5:14).

We worship a God who is omnipresent and omnipotent. He hears and answers our prayers anytime, anyplace. What does it mean to pray continually? It means that we are God-conscious at all times. We carry on a continuous dialogue with God. Whatever we see or hear or experience becomes a subject of prayer.

I used to ride my bicycle with friends on the Silver Comet Trail, a biking and running trail that winds through Georgia (named for the *Silver Comet* passenger train that used to travel that route). One day my friends and I came upon the scene of a bicycle accident. An ambulance had driven out on the narrow trail and the paramedics were tending to an injured cyclist on the ground. I said, "Let's stop and pray for this man."

One of my friends said, "But we don't who he is."

I said, "That makes no difference. The Lord knows him."

To pray continually means to be keenly, constantly aware of God's presence—and our need for unceasing surrender to his will.

When we learn of a need, we stop and pray.

When we face a challenge, we ask God for wisdom and strength.

When we experience a blessing, we pause to give thanks.

When there is evil or injustice, we cry out to God.

When we encounter an unbelieving neighbor, we ask God for an opening and boldness to witness.

Prayer is spiritual respiration. It should be as regular, continual, and automatic as the breaths we take—breathe in, breathe out.

PRAY IN THE SPIRIT

Paul uses a phrase in Ephesians 6:18 that we should examine more closely: "*Pray in the Spirit* on all occasions..." What does the phrase "pray in the Spirit" mean?

Many of our Pentecostal friends say that praying in the Spirit means "speaking in tongues." But that is not what Paul means. To pray in the Spirit means to pray in concert with, and under the guidance of, the Holy Spirit. It means to pray in the name of Jesus and in accordance with the will of Jesus. If you pray in the Spirit, you will not ask for things that are contrary to the Word of God or the will of God.

There is a passage in Paul's letter to the Romans that has always been a great comfort to me. I have practiced this form of prayer more times than I can count: "In the same way, the Spirit helps us in our weakness. We do not know what we ought to pray for, but the Spirit himself intercedes for us through wordless groans. And he who searches our hearts knows the mind of the Spirit, because the Spirit intercedes for God's people in accordance with the will of God" (Romans 8:26-27).

To pray in the Spirit is to be in harmony with the Holy Spirit. It means that we pray in subjection and submission to the Holy Spirit. It means that we are in continuous conversation with God through the Holy Spirit, every hour, every day.

All too many Christians are never serious about prayer until a problem arises. We treat prayer like one of those fire extinguisher boxes with the red lettering that reads, "In Case of Emergency, Break Glass." We pray as if we expect God to say, "Nine-one-one, state your emergency."

Yes, prayer *is* for emergencies, but not *only* for emergencies. A key truth bears repeating: Prayer should be the very air we breathe.

You might say, "You're being unrealistic, Michael. How can I pray when I'm driving or working or watching the news?" Please try it! "Lord, give me wisdom to drive safely." "Lord, help me to be a witness to my coworkers." "Lord, please bring peace and your gospel to that troubled region."

Once you begin to see prayer not as an occasional pause with God but as an unbroken, unending conversation with God, your experience of prayer will be revolutionized. If you are used to praying only in times of need or emergency, it might help to remember that you are in an invisible war. You might find yourself under spiritual attack at any moment. So there is always a need for prayer. There is always the possibility of a spiritual emergency.

Remember Paul's words: "With this in mind, *be alert* and *always keep on praying* for all the Lord's people." He gives this word of counsel to the Ephesians in the context of spiritual warfare and right after he has urged them to put on the full armor of God. This is a call to remain on a continuous war footing and always be ready for battle. Praying in the Spirit means maintaining a state of spiritual watchfulness, readiness, and awareness of Satan's schemes.

INTERCEDING FOR OTHERS

I find it fascinating that, in these verses on prayer in Ephesians 6, Paul does not mention how he prays for himself. Instead, he asks the Ephesian believers to pray for him. He writes, "Pray also for me, that whenever I speak, words may be given me so that I will fearlessly make known the mystery of the gospel, for which I am an ambassador in chains. Pray that I may declare it fearlessly, as I should" (Ephesians 6:19-20).

The healthiest, most powerful prayer life is one that is devoted to intercession for others. I feel more blessed when I'm praying for other people than you can imagine. A self-absorbed, self-obsessed prayer life is weak and ineffectual because it is not praying in the Spirit. The Spirit of God brings love for others, compassion for others, concern for others. A strong and vibrant prayer life is not focused on "my wants" and "my agenda." It's not focused on "me" at all. It's focused on the spiritual welfare of others. It's focused on God's agenda, the kingdom agenda.

When Jesus said, "Seek first his kingdom and his righteousness, and all these things will be given to you as well" (Matthew 6:33), he was laying out God's priority in prayer. He was telling us that our foremost priority should be aligning our lives with God's purposes and his righteous character. The Lord's directive not only shapes how we should live, but also how we should pray.

By seeking God's kingdom first in prayer, we prioritize his will over our own desires. When we ask God to advance his kingdom in our lives, prayer becomes less about our personal wish list and more about reporting for duty.

Seeking God's kingdom involves praying for others in ways that reflect God's priorities. It means praying not merely for our loved ones' material needs and protection but also for their spiritual growth and the reign of God's justice and mercy in their lives. The Lord's promise that "all these things will be given to you as well" assures us that he knows and cares for our earthly needs.

Intercessory prayer is one of the most beautiful, meaningful, life-changing aspects of the Christian life. I pray for you, and you pray for me. As we pray, we both seek first the kingdom of God and his righteousness. That is the highest form of praying in the Spirit.

Paul wrote the letter to the Ephesians while he was in a Roman prison in around AD 62. Notice that Paul did not ask his Ephesian friends to pray for the healing of his sore, shackled ankles. He didn't ask them to pray for his release from prison. No, Paul's primary concern was for the proclamation of the gospel. His plea is a prayer for the expansion of the kingdom of God. His passion is for lost people to come to know Jesus Christ as their Lord and Savior.

THE FEARS OF THE FEARLESS APOSTLE

Why did Paul ask his Ephesian friends to pray "that I may declare [the gospel] fearlessly, as I should"? As we read the story of his missionary journeys in Acts and as we read his letters, he appears to be the most fearless person in the New Testament, other than the Lord Jesus himself. Doesn't this seem like a strange prayer request for the courageous missionary apostle to make?

In my personal opinion (and it's *only* my personal opinion), Paul must have experienced times when he was tempted to be quiet about Jesus, times when he felt tempted to mute the message of salvation, times when he felt tempted to compromise God's Word, in order to get out of prison. After all, why would he ask them to pray for his boldness if he did not feel tempted to keep silent?

I interpret this passage as Paul's plea that believers would intercede on his behalf—a plea that they would petition God to aid him in overcoming the temptation toward fear and timidity. He was asking his brothers and sisters to pray for the strength to withstand Satan's attempt to intimidate him into silence or compromise.

Paul did not ask to be set free from his prison cell or his chains. His discomforts were incidental to him. What he wanted most was victory over temptation. Spiritual victory meant more to him than physical freedom.

God cannot use a self-sufficient person. The reason God was able to use Paul in such a mighty way, leading so many people to Christ and planting so many churches, is that he did not try to do everything in his own strength. He lived in absolute dependence upon God's strength. He knew he could accomplish nothing unless he was lifted up and carried along by the prayers of God's people.

If the apostle Paul recognized his need of the prayers of God's people, who are we to think we can get along fine without those prayers? Paul asked for intercessory prayer because he knew that Satan targets spiritual leaders—pastors, missionaries, teachers, elders, and lay leaders—for destruction. Satan wants to topple the shepherds so that the sheep are left vulnerable and discouraged.

Even in prison, Paul's sole concern, his only prayer request, is for the impact of the gospel of Jesus Christ. When he called himself "an ambassador in chains" for the gospel, he meant that literally. He saw himself as an accredited ambassador, representing the Lord Jesus Christ at the imperial court of Rome. Paul was proud to be an ambassador of Jesus Christ—even though he was an ambassador in chains.

Notice the irony in that phrase, "ambassador in chains." Now, it was not unusual for the noblemen and noblewomen of Rome, nor the ambassadors from other provinces and nations, to wear chains—sparkling gold chains of precious jewelry—around their necks and wrists. They wore glittering golden chains to show off their wealth, power, and prestige.

But whoever heard of an ambassador wearing the cruel, heavy chains of a prisoner?

Paul was the ambassador of the crucified Christ. He was a fearless warrior in the invisible war. From his prison cell, he wrote this great document, the letter to the Ephesians, which lays out God's strategy for fighting and winning this spiritual war. And the key element of that strategy is prayer.

So, as we near the end of this book, let me pose a few questions. Let me ask you:

Do your priorities align with the kingdom priorities of God? Do you have a passion for sharing the gospel and advancing the kingdom of God in your neighborhood and your workplace? In your prayer life, and especially in your intercession for others, do you seek first the kingdom of God and his righteousness?

Maintain constant communication with your Commander. He has already won the invisible war on that hill where he declared, "It is finished!" Breathe out your requests in prayer. Breathe in his wisdom and strength. Then go forth into the spiritual battles of this life with faith and confidence in him.

If you are a Christian believer, I have some encouragement for you. I want to send you out into the world with a word of inspiration and empowerment as you fight your spiritual battles. Remember, as a follower of Jesus, you have everything you need to be victorious in the invisible war. You are a warrior of the cross—and your faithful obedience to Jesus makes the devil tremble.

CONCLUSION

STAND FIRM TO THE END

Let's close this book with two stories. If you have doubts about your salvation, if you aren't certain that you'll live forever in eternity with Jesus, this first story is for you. It's a story from my boyhood.

When I was four or five years old, I was rebellious and uncontrollable. I was constantly running away from home. My parents and older siblings tried everything they could think of to stop me, but I was too determined and too quick on my feet.

At the time, my parents owned a four-story building, and we lived on the top floor. Every time I ran away from home, I had to run down four flights of stairs as fast as I could, and then dash out the front door. Once I was in the street, I could vanish into the crowd, and then sprint off in any direction. I liked to explore the streets, visit the shops, and hang out with friends without anyone telling me what to do.

My parents would send my siblings out in search parties. They would comb the streets and try to figure out where I was headed. If they found me and dragged me home, my parents would impose punishments on me that would have reformed any other child—but they had no effect on me.

In those days, there was a homeless man who prowled around

the neighborhood. He dressed shabbily. He acted strangely. There were wild rumors about him. All the kids were afraid of him and kept their distance from him. We called him "the hobo." That strange man inspired my oldest brother, Samir, with a plan to teach me not to run away.

One day, I was at the top of the stairs, planning my next escape. I looked in every direction. When I was sure no one was watching, I took off down the stairs like a streaking meteor. I reached the bottom landing and saw the front door before me. There was no one to stop me.

As I dashed toward the door—*blam!*—the door of the storage room to my left flung open. A shabbily dressed man jumped out at me. He snarled and put his arms out to grab me.

I shrieked in terror. Eluding his grasp, I turned and dashed up all four flights of stairs in record time, slamming the door behind me. My heart hammered faster than a hummingbird's wings.

Of course, the shabbily dressed man was Samir. But I was certain he was the scary hobo who prowled our neighborhood.

I never ran away again.

IT'S TIME TO STOP RUNNING

I'm sure the point of this story is obvious. If you are running away from God, if you're trying to avoid being obedient to his Word, you are only leaving yourself open to the enemy's attack. Rebellion opens the door wide to the enemy. Disobedience will bring you pain, fear, and suffering. Why? Because you have left yourself defenseless. The farther you run away, the longer your trip home.

Don't think that the invisible war won't sweep you up and destroy you. If you are running from God, you are in constant danger. Please don't run away. Stay close to your loving Father. Let him keep you safe. Run home into his protective embrace.

If you have never invited Jesus to be your Lord and Savior, I urge you to do so right now. In Luke 15, Jesus tells two stories that might describe your life right now. He tells a story about a shepherd who has lost one of his 100 sheep; he leaves the 99 to search for the lost sheep until he finds it. Jesus also tells a story about a woman who had ten silver coins—then she lost one; she searched diligently until she found that one lost coin.

Jesus explained the meaning of those two stories: "In the same way, I tell you, there is rejoicing in the presence of the angels of God over one sinner who repents" (Luke 15:10). God desires that you be found, not lost. He's not willing to save *some* sheep, *some* coins, *some* souls, and let others be lost. He wants a relationship with you. He loves you with an infinite, unconditional love, and he longs for you to accept the forgiveness he offers. If you are willing to receive the gift of salvation right now, then please pray this prayer with all your heart:

> *Father, I confess that I am a sinner. I have not loved you with my whole heart. I have not kept your commandments or sought a relationship with you. I believe Jesus canceled my debt of sin through his death on the cross. I accept him as my Lord and Savior. I accept your forgiveness. Have mercy on me and forgive me, I pray. Help me to live the rest of my life in gratitude for all you have done for me. In Jesus's name, amen.*

If you prayed that prayer, then you've made the most important decision of your life. I urge you to tell someone—your husband or wife, your parents, or some Christian friends. Begin reading the Bible. Find a church that teaches the Bible as God's Word. Begin growing in your daily walk with the Lord Jesus.

THE POWER OF PERSEVERANCE

Finally, if you are a Christian believer, I have some encouragement for you. I want to send you out into the world with a word of inspiration and empowerment as you fight your spiritual battles. Remember, as a follower of Jesus, you have everything you need to be victorious in the invisible war. You are a warrior of the cross—and your faithful obedience to Jesus makes the devil tremble.

So be strong in the Lord and in his mighty power! Put on the full armor of God. Take your stand against Satan's schemes. Remember that you are standing in the heavenly realms alongside Jesus himself. Keep the lines of communication open at all times. Pray in the Spirit for all of God's people. Share the good news of Jesus Christ with everyone around you and declare it fearlessly! And no matter how tough the opposition may seem, no matter how fiercely the enemy attacks, never give up on Jesus. Persevere—and he will win the battle for you.

In that spirit, here's the final story. It's the true story of a woman named Florence Chadwick. On the morning of July 4, 1952, Chadwick waded into the water near Catalina Island. Her plan was to swim across the channel to the California coast, a distance of 26 miles. Chadwick was a strong and experienced swimmer (she was the first woman to cross the English Channel both ways).

Several chase boats accompanied her for her safety. As she stepped into the waves, the water was surprisingly cold for July. The fog was so thick that she could hardly see the boats that were tracking her. She began to swim in strong, steady strokes.

Hour after hour, she swam. The farther she went, the thicker the fog became. Chadwick feared that she might be swimming in circles. Her mother—who was also her trainer—was in one of the boats, calling words of encouragement to her. After 15 hours in the water, Chadwick called to her support crew and asked to be pulled into the boat.

She later learned that she had swum 25.5 miles. She had quit just half a mile from the shore.

The following day, she told reporters, "All I could see was the fog...I think if I could have seen the shore, I would have made it."[1]

Friend in Christ, I can assure you of this: Satan has a fog machine. If he can confuse you, discourage you, and cause you to despair, he will crank out more fog than you can imagine. He will keep you in a fog about God's promises. He will keep you in a fog about the truth of Jesus and his resurrection and your salvation. He will keep you in a fog about God's will for your life.

When you realize that you are in a fog of doubt, discouragement, and despondency, remember Florence Chadwick. She swam 25.5 miles of a 26-mile journey. In other words, she had successfully traveled 98.08 percent of the distance—and then she gave up.

No matter what you are going through, no matter how discouraging your circumstances, remember Florence Chadwick's words: "All I could see was the fog." If all you can see is the fog right now, remember that she was less than 2 percent of the way from shore.

Ask God to dispel the fog and light your way home. Ask him to turn your doubt into faith, your discouragement into hope, and your despondency into strength. Remember that the invisible war has already been won by the Lord Jesus Christ on the cross.

The fog that surrounds you now is temporary. It will vanish when you turn your eyes upon Jesus, the Son of the living God. He is our great Commander and Conqueror, and he will lead you to victory and peace.

NOTES

INTRODUCTION—THE STRUGGLE WE FACE

1. Lizzie O'Leary, "Russia's Invisible War on Ukraine," Slate.com, February 25, 2022, https://slate.com/technology/2022/02/ukraine-russia-cyberwar-sandworm-gru.html.

2. The Barna Group, "Most American Christians Do Not Believe that Satan or the Holy Spirit Exist," Barna.com, April 13, 2009, https://www.barna.com/research/most-american-christians-do-not-believe-that-satan-or-the-holy-spirit-exist/.

3. David Cortright, *Peace: A History of Movements and Ideas* (Cambridge, UK: Cambridge University Press, 2008), 164-165.

4. Phil Ochs, "Draft Dodger Rag," lyrics at Genius.com, https://genius.com/Phil-ochs-draft-dodger-rag-lyrics.

CHAPTER 1—ASSAULT FROM THE OUTSIDE

1. Sarah Al-Arshani. "ACLU Hails First 'After-School Satan Club' Meeting at Virginia Elementary School 'A Victory for Free Speech and Religious Liberty.'" *Business Insider*, February 18, 2023, https://www.businessinsider.com/first-after-school-satan-club-meeting-held-virginia-elementary-school-2023-2; Katherine Stewart, "An After School Satan Club Could Be Coming to Your Kid's Elementary School," *Washington Post*, July 30, 2016, https://www.washingtonpost.com/local/education/an-after-school-satan-club-could-be-coming-to-your-kids-elementary-school/2016/07/30/63f485e6-5427-11e6-88eb-7dda4e2f2aec_story.html.

2. C.S. Lewis, *The Screwtape Letters* (New York: Macmillan, 1954), 39-40.

3. Massachusetts Department of Children and Families, *Annual Report FY2022, Descriptive and Outcome Data: FY2018-FY2022*, The Commonwealth of Massachusetts, Executive Office of Health and Human Services, Department of Children and Families, December 2022, https://www.mass.gov/doc/fy-2022/download.

4. Kathy Curran, "DCF Struggling Without Enough Foster Homes," WCVB Channel 5, January 17, 2019, https://www.wcvb.com/article/dcf-struggling-without-enough-foster-homes/25921664.

5. Will Hall, "UK's Foremost Expert: Gender Ideology Is 'A Cult Belief,'" Baptistmessage.com, May 30, 2023, https://www.baptistmessage.com/uks-foremost-expert-gender-ideology-is-made-up/.

6. Kathleen Hayes, "Gender Ideology's True Believers," May 19, 2022, https://quillette.com/2022/05/19/gender-ideologys-true-believers/.

7. Isabela Espadas Barros Leal, "Massachusetts Couple Denied Foster Care Application Over LGBTQ Views, Complaint Says," NBC News, August 10, 2023, https://www.nbcnews.com/nbc-out/out-news/massachusetts-couple-denied-foster-care-application-lgbtq-views-compla-rcna99339.

8. Heritage Foundation, "Poll: Americans are Wary of Gender Identity and Sexual Orientation Ideology and Policy's Impact on Minors," Heritage.org, February 2021, https://www.heritage.org/sites/default/files/2021-02/SOGI_Minors_OnePager.pdf.

9. President Joseph R. Biden, "Executive Order on Preventing and Combating Discrimination on the Basis of Gender Identity or Sexual Orientation," The White House, Briefing Room. Presidential Actions, January 20, 2021, https://www.federalregister.gov/documents/2021/01/25/2021-01761/preventing-and-combating-discrimination-on-the-basis-of-gender-identity-or-sexual-orientation.

10. Christopher F. Rufo. "Suppression Campaign." City Journal, October 12, 2022, https://www.city-journal.org/article/suppression-campaign.

11. Erin McCormick, "'Are You a Boy or a Girl'? Drag Queen Story Hour Riles the Right, but Delights Kids," *The Guardian*, June 13, 2017, https://www.theguardian.com/world/2017/jun/13/drag-queen-story-hour-library-books-children-gender; Valerie Richardson, "Drag Queen Story Hours for Children Grow Across the U.S. So Does the Backlash," *Washington Times*, January 1, 2023, https://www.washingtontimes.com/news/2023/jan/1/drag-queen-story-hours-children-grow-across-us-so-/.

12. Drag Story Hour staff, "Drag Story Hour," DragStoryHour.org, no posting date, https://www.dragstoryhour.org/.

13. These organizations appeared on DragStoryHour.org as of March 24, 2025.

14. Movieguide Staff, "How Walt Disney's Faith Was Central to His Groundbreaking Career in Entertainment," Movieguide.org, no posting date, https://www.movieguide.org/news-articles/how-walt-disneys-faith-was-central-to-his-groundbreaking-career-in-entertainment.html.

15. Wikipedia, "Disney and LGBTQ Representation in Animation," Wikipedia.org, updated January 25, 2025, https://en.wikipedia.org/wiki/Disney_and_LGBTQ_representation_in_animation.

16. Caroline Downey, "Disney Executive Producer Admits to 'Gay Agenda,' 'Adding Queerness' Wherever She Could," *National Review*, March 29, 2022, https://www.nationalreview.com/news/disney-executive-producer-admits-to-gay-agenda-adding-queerness-wherever-she-could/.

17. Andrew C. McCarthy, "The Wrong Way to Fight Progressive Indoctrination in Public Schools," *National Review*, October 25, 2021, https://www.nationalreview.com/2021/10/the-wrong-way-to-fight-progressive-indoctrination-in-public-schools/.

18. Kaylee McGhee White, "Americans Know Public Schools Are Indoctrinating Their Children," *Washington Examiner*, August 19, 2022, https://www.washingtonexaminer.com/news/2873751/americans-know-public-schools-are-indoctrinating-their-children/. [Note: The *1619 Project* teaches that America was founded *not* in 1776, but in 1619, when the first slaves arrived—and that America was founded to benefit and protect the slave trade. The *Gender Unicorn*, published by Trans Student Educational Resources, indoctrinates children into the notion of "spectrums of gender and sexuality."]

19. Kaylee McGhee White, "Americans Know Public Schools Are Indoctrinating Their Children."

20. Kali Fontanilla, "I'm a Teacher. Here's How My School Tried to Indoctrinate Children," Orange County Register, February 14, 2022, https://www.ocregister.com/2022/02/14/im-a-teacher-heres-how-my-school-tried-to-indoctrinate-children/.

21. Tian An, "Can Mathematics Be Antiracist?," AMS Blogs, January 31, 2020, https://blogs.ams.org/inclusionexclusion/2020/01/31/can-mathematics-be-antiracist/.

22. Jay Caspian Kang, "The Anti-C.R.T. Movement and a Vision For a New Right Wing," New York Times, February 10, 2022, https://www.nytimes.com/2022/02/10/opinion/anti-crt-politics.html; Hana Yamahiro and Luna Garzón-Montano, "A Mirage Not a Movement: The Misguided Enterprise of Progressive Prosecution," N.Y.U. Review of Law & Social Change, no posting date, https://socialchangenyu.com/harbinger/a-mirage-not-a-movement-the-misguided-enterprise-of-progressive-prosecution/.

23. Hannah Grossman, "Alvin Bragg Promises Not to Prosecute Theft to Establish 'Racial Equity' Balance: 'Crime of Poverty,'" FoxNews.com, April 20, 2023, https://www.foxnews.com/media/alvin-bragg-promises-not-prosecute-theft-establish-racial-equity-agenda-crime-poverty.

24. Hannah Grossman, "DA Alvin Bragg's Chief Prosecutor Said Criminals Aren't 'Bad Dudes,' Ripped 'Racist' Justice System," FoxNews.com, March 28, 2023, https://www.foxnews.com/media/da-alvin-braggs-chief-prosecutor-criminals-arent-bad-dudes-ripped-racist-justice-system.

25. Hannah Grossman, "Alvin Bragg's Chief Prosecutor Brags about Giving Get-Out-of-Jail Free Cards to Violent Felons, Murderer," FoxNews.com, April 5, 2023, https://www.foxnews.com/media/alvin-braggs-chief-prosecutor-brags-giving-get-out-jail-free-cards-violent-felons-muderer.

26. Cully Stimson and Zack Smith, "Meet Alvin Bragg, Rogue Prosecutor Whose Policies Are Wreaking Havoc in Manhattan," Daily Signal, January 28, 2022, https://www.dailysignal.com/2022/01/28/meet-alvin-bragg-rogue-prosecutor-whose-policies-are-wreaking-havoc-in-manhattan; Morgan Phillips, "Exclusive: New York Bodega Clerk Wrongfully Charged with Murder for Stabbing Attacker and Mother Whose Son was Stabbed to Death Lead GOP Witnesses for Judiciary Hearing Targeting Alvin Bragg," House Judiciary Committee, April 12, 2023, https://judiciary.house.gov/media/in-the-news/exclusive-new-york-bodega-clerk-wrongfully-charged-murder-stabbing-attacker-and; Matthew Sedacca, "Bodega Clerk Jose Alba Sues Manhattan DA Alvin Bragg, NYPD for Racial Discrimination," New York Post, September 30, 2023, https://nypost.com/2023/09/30/nyc-bodega-worker-jose-alba-sues-da-alvin-bragg-nypd/.

27. Hurubie Meko and Anusha Bayya, "Daniel Penny Is Acquitted in Death of Jordan Neely on Subway," New York Times, December 9, 2024, https://www.nytimes.com/2024/12/09/nyregion/daniel-penny-not-guilty-jordan-neely.html; Khaleda Rahman, "Jordan Neely's Criminal Record: Man Killed on Subway Had 42 Prior Arrests," Newsweek, May 4, 2023, https://www.newsweek.com/jordan-neely-arrest-record-outrage-grows-subway-death-1798248; Stepheny Price, "Critics Warn of 'Daniel Penny Effect' After Woman Burned Alive on NYC Subway Car as Bystanders Watched," FoxNews.com, December 24, 2024, https://www.foxnews.com/us/critics-warn-daniel-penny-effect-after-woman-burned-alive-nyc-subway-car-bystanders-watched.

28. Cully Stimson and Zack Smith, "Meet Alvin Bragg, Rogue Prosecutor Whose Policies Are Wreaking Havoc in Manhattan," Daily Signal, January 28, 2022, https://www.dailysignal.com/2022/01/28/meet-alvin-bragg-rogue-prosecutor-whose-policies-are-wreaking-havoc-in-manhattan.

29. Joshua Rhett Miller, "BLM Site Removes Page on 'Nuclear Family Structure' Amid NFL Vet's Criticism," New York Post, September 24, 2020, https://nypost.com/2020/09/24/blm-removes-website-language-blasting-nuclear-family-structure/; Mike Gonzalez, "Socialism and Family," Heritage.org, March 1, 2022, https://www.heritage.org/marriage-and-family/commentary/socialism-and-family.

30. Lois Beckett, "At Least 25 Americans Were Killed During Protests and Political Unrest in 2020," The Guardian, October 31, 2020, https://www.theguardian.com/world/2020/oct/31/americans-killed-protests-political-unrest-acled.

31. Jennifer A. Kingson, "Exclusive: $1 Billion-Plus Riot Damage Is Most Expensive in Insurance History, Axios.com, September 16, 2020, https://www.axios.com/2020/09/16/riots-cost-property-damage.

32. James Jeffrey, "Perhaps Black Lives Matter Was Right About The Nuclear Family," The Critic,

December 9, 2020, https://thecritic.co.uk/perhaps-black-lives-matter-was-right-about-the-nuclear-family/; Joshua Rhett Miller, "BLM Site Removes Page on 'Nuclear Family Structure' amid NFL Vet's Criticism," *New York Post*, September 24, 2020, https://nypost.com/2020/09/24/blm-removes-website-language-blasting-nuclear-family-structure/.

33. Karl Marx, *The Communist Manifesto*, "Chapter II. Proletarians and Communists," Marxists.org, https://www.marxists.org/archive/marx/works/1848/communist-manifesto/ch02.htm.

34. Stephane Courtois, Nicolas Werth, Jean-Louis Panne, Andrzej Paczkowski, Karel Bartosek, Jean-Louis Margolin, *The Black Book of Communism: Crimes, Terror, Repression* (Cambridge, MA: Harvard University Press, 1999), xi.

35. Dionne Searcey and Madison Malone Kircher, "Torrent of Hate for Health Insurance Industry Follows C.E.O.'s Killing," *New York Times*, December 5, 2024, https://www.nytimes.com/2024/12/05/nyregion/social-media-insurance-industry-brian-thompson.html.

36. Igor Bobic, " 'This Is A Warning': Warren, Sanders Address Sympathy For UnitedHealthcare CEO Killing," *Huffington Post*, December 10, 2024, https://www.huffpost.com/entry/warren-sanders-brian-thompson-health-care_n_6758bc0fe4b063b52a9a524b.

37. Filip Timotija, "Shock Poll: 41 Percent of Young Voters Find Killing of UnitedHealthcare CEO Acceptable," *The Hill*, December 17, 2024, https://thehill.com/policy/healthcare/5044269-poll-finds-41-percent-find-killing-unacceptable/.

CHAPTER 2—THE BATTLE WITHIN

1. PBS / WNET New York, "Freedom: A History of US / Biography: George B. McClellan," Thirteen PBS, no posting date, https://www.thirteen.org/wnet/historyofus/web06/features/bio/B06.html.

2. American Battlefield Trust staff, "George B. McClellan," American Battlefield Trust (Battlefields.org), no posting date, https://www.battlefields.org/learn/biographies/george-b-mcclellan.

3. Christian History Institute staff, "God's Wonderful Working," Christian History Institute, originally published in *Christian History*, No. 23, 1989, no posting date, https://christianhistoryinstitute.org/magazine/article/gods-wonderful-working.

CHAPTER 3—ANGELS AND DEMONS

1. C. Peter Wagner, *Prayer Shield: How to Intercede for Pastors and Christian Leaders* (Ventura CA: Regal, 2014), 66-67.

2. Michael D. Davis, "Amid Outcry, Satanic Temple of Iowa Hosts Reading Marathon on Tama County Courthouse Lawn," *Times-Republican* (Marshalltown, IA), September 19, 2024, https://www.timesrepublican.com/news/todays-news/2024/09/amid-outcry-satanic-temple-of-iowa-hosts-reading-marathon-on-tama-county-courthouse-lawn/.

3. Kaylee Olivas, " 'We Will Put Satanists In The Schools': The Satanic Temple to Send Ministers to OK if Bill Allowing School Chaplains Is Signed into Law," KFOR News 4, April 30, 2024, https://kfor.com/news/local/we-will-put-satanists-in-the-schools-the-satanic-temple-to-send-ministers-to-ok-if-bill-allowing-school-chaplains-is-signed-into-law/; Richard Luscombe, "Satanists to Volunteer in Florida Schools in Protest at Desantis Religious Bill," *The Guardian*, July 8, 2024, https://www.theguardian.com/us-news/article/2024/jul/08/florida-satanic-temple-ron-desantis.

4. Caroline Cummings, Riley Moser, WCCO Staff, "Satanists' Holiday Display at Minnesota Capitol Sparks Outrage," CBS News, December 18, 2024, https://www.cbsnews.com/minnesota/news/minnesota-capitol-satanic-holiday-display/; Molly Farrar, "New

Hampshire Capital Includes Satanists in Nativity Scene 'To Avoid Litigation,'" Boston .com, December 9, 2024, https://www.boston.com/news/local-news/2024/12/09/new-hampshire-capital-includes-satanists-in-nativity-scene-to-avoid-litigation/.

5. For example, Psalm 24:10 in the King James Version reads, "Who is this King of glory? The LORD of hosts, he is the King of glory." For some reason, the New International Version does not use the phrase "the LORD of hosts," but uses the phrase "the LORD Almighty" instead. I think this was an unfortunate choice by the translators, because it fails to convey the fact that God is truly the Commander of innumerable hosts of angels.

CHAPTER 4—ARMORED FOR BATTLE

1. Office of Public Affairs, Department of Justice, "Former Second Chance Body Armor President Settles False Claims Act Case Related to Defective Bullet Proof Vests," Justice.gov, July 16, 2018, https://www.justice.gov/opa/pr/former-second-chance-body-armor-president-settles-false-claims-act-case-related-defective; Goldberg Kohn Blog, "Second Chance Body Armor—A False Claims Act Case Study," WhistleblowersAttorneys.com, April 27, 2023, https://www.whistleblowersattorneys.com/blog/second-chance-body-armor-a-false-claims-act-case-study/.

CHAPTER 6—THE BLESSINGS OF SURRENDER

1. James Balmont, "Onoda: The Man Who Hid in the Jungle for 30 Years," BBC.com, April 13, 2022, https://www.bbc.com/culture/article/20220413-onoda-the-man-who-hid-in-the-jungle-for-30-years; James Barber, "One Japanese Soldier Continued to Fight for 30 Years After WWII," Military.com, December 14, 2022, https://www.military.com/off-duty/movies/2022/12/14/one-japanese-soldier-continued-fight-30-years-after-wwii.html.

2. A.W. Tozer, *That Incredible Christian* (Wheaton, IL: Tyndale, 1964), 11-12.

3. J. Hudson Taylor, "The Source of Power," speech delivered at Carnegie Hall, New York City, April 23, 1900, Prevailing Intercessory Prayer, no posting date, https://www.path2prayer.com/famous-christians-their-lives-and-writings-including-free-books/j-hudson-taylor-pioneer-missionary-to-china/hudson-taylor-source-of-power.

4. Jessica Brain, "William Booth and the Salvation Army," Historic UK, no posting date, https://www.historic-uk.com/CultureUK/William-Booth-Salvation-Army/; Salvation Army staff, "William Booth," Salvation Army UK, no posting date, https://www.salvationarmy.org.uk/about-us/international-heritage-centre/virtual-heritage-centre/people/william-booth.

CHAPTER 7—KNOW YOUR ENEMY

1. Martin H. Manser, ed., *The Westminster Collection of Christian Quotations* (Louisville, KY: Westminster John Knox Press, 2001), 72.

CHAPTER 8—WIELDING YOUR SWORD

1. Louis Casiano, "Incoming California Congressman to Be Sworn in on U.S. Constitution, Superman Comic," FoxNews.com, January 3, 2023, https://www.foxnews.com/politics/california-congressman-sworn-superman-comic.

2. Lauren Everitt and Chi Chi Izundu, "Who, What, Why: How Long Can Someone Survive Without Food?," BBC News, February 20, 2012, https://www.bbc.com/news/magazine-17095605.

CHAPTER 9—RECOVERY FROM FAILURE

1. David MacIsaac and the Editors of *Encyclopedia Britannica*, "World History >Wars, Battles & Armed Conflicts >Strategic Bombing," Britannica Online, August 23, 1998, https://www.britannica.com/topic/air-warfare.

2. K.R. Singh, "Air-Power Strategy and Ground Support Operations in High Altitude," *Strategic Analysis: A Monthly Journal of the IDSA*, July 2000, https://ciaotest.cc.columbia.edu/olj/sa/sa_jul00sik01.html.

CHAPTER 10—DON'T FORGET TO BREATHE

1. Our Daily Bread, "John Knox," Bible.org, no posting date, https://bible.org/illustration/john-knox.

2. John Bunyan, *The Pilgrim's Progress: From This World to That Which Is to Come*, Part One, sections 135-136, https://www.gutenberg.org/cache/epub/131/pg131-images.html.

3. James Russell Lowell, "Vision of Sir Launfal," the digital collection American Verse Project, University of Michigan Library Digital Collections, https://name.umdl.umich.edu/BAP5378.0001.001.

4. John R. W. Stott, *The Message of Ephesians*, Revised Edition (Downers Grove, IL: InterVarsity Press, 2020), 227.

5. John Bunyan, *The Pilgrim's Progress*, section 161.

CONCLUSION—STAND FIRM TO THE END

1. David R. Smith, "Florence's Fog," It's Like This, https://www.itslikethis.org/florences-fog/; Randy Alcorn, "Florence Chadwick and the Fog," Eternal Perspective Ministries, January 21, 2010, https://www.epm.org/resources/2010/Jan/21/florence-chadwick-and-fog/.

OTHER HARVEST HOUSE BOOKS BY MICHAEL YOUSSEF

Conquer

Fearless Living in Troubled Times

God, Help Me Overcome My Circumstances

God, Help Me Rebuild My Broken World

God, Just Tell Me What to Do

Leading the Way Through Daniel

Leading the Way Through Ephesians

Leading the Way Through Galatians

Leading the Way Through Joshua

My Refuge, My Strength

The Leadership Style of Jesus

To learn more about Harvest House books and
to read sample chapters, visit our website:

www.HarvestHousePublishers.com

HARVEST HOUSE PUBLISHERS
EUGENE, OREGON